THE FORGE

St Josemaría Escrivá

THE FORGE

SCEPTER

London New York

This edition is published:
in England by Scepter (U.K.) Ltd., 21 Hinton Avenue, Hounslow TW4 6AP; e-mail: scepter@pobox.com;
in the United States by Scepter Publishers Inc.; 800-322-8773; e-mail: info@scepterpublishers.org; www.scepterpublishers.org

With ecclesiastical approval
ISBN: 978-1-910644-09-6

Typeset by MI Intermedia, and printed in Singapore.

CONTENTS

The Author

St Josemaría Escrivá de Balaguer was born in Barbastro, in northern Spain, on 9 January 1902. At the age of 15 or 16 he began to feel the first intimations that God was calling him and he decided to become a priest. He started his ecclesiastical studies in the Seminary of Logroño in 1918, and later, in 1920, in that of St Francis de Paula in Saragossa, where from 1922 he was a superior or tutor. In 1923 he began to study Civil Law in the University of Saragossa, with the permission of his ecclesiastical superiors. These studies did not interfere with his theological studies. He was ordained deacon on 20 December 1924 and became a priest on 28 March 1925.

He began his work as a priest in the

village of Perdiguera, within the diocese of Saragossa, and afterwards in Saragossa itself. In the spring of 1927, with the permission of the Archbishop of Saragossa, he moved to the Spanish capital, Madrid, and there carried out abundant priestly work among all kinds of people, devoting attention also to the poor and destitute in the outlying districts of the city, and especially to the incurably sick and the dying in the hospitals. He worked as chaplain to the *Patronato de Enfermos* (Foundation for the Sick), a welfare organisation run by the Apostolic Sisters of the Sacred Heart. He also taught at a university academy, and continued his studies for a doctorate in Civil Law, which at that time could only be obtained from the University of Madrid.

On 2 October 1928 God made him *see* clearly what up to then he had only had inklings of; and St Josemaría Escrivá founded Opus Dei (in English, the Work of God). Under God's continuing guidance, on 14 February 1930 he understood that he must open up the apostolic work of Opus Dei to women also. As a result, a new path was opening up in the Church, to promote, among people of all social classes, the search for holiness and the practice of the apostolate, through the sanctification of ordinary work, in the midst of the world and without changing one's state in life.

From 2 October 1928, the Founder of Opus Dei directed his energies to the mission God had entrusted to him, with great apostolic zeal for all souls. In 1934 he was appointed Rector of the *Patronato de Santa Isabel* (St Elizabeth Foundation). During the Spanish Civil War, at times putting his life at risk, he carried out his priestly ministry in Madrid and, subsequently, in the northern city of Burgos. Already in those years St Josemaría Escrivá experienced harsh and sustained opposition, which he bore calmly and with a supernatural outlook.

On 14 February 1943 he founded the Priestly Society of the Holy Cross, which is inseparably united to Opus Dei and which, as well as opening up the possibility of ordaining lay members of Opus Dei to the priesthood and incardinating them for the service of the Work, would later on also enable priests who are incardinated in dioceses to share the spirituality and asceticism of Opus

Dei, seeking holiness in the exercise of their ministerial duties, while remaining exclusively under their respective Ordinaries.

In 1946 he took up residence in Rome, which was to be his home for the rest of his life. From there, he stimulated and guided the development of Opus Dei throughout the world, using all his energies to give to the men and women of Opus Dei a solid formation in doctrine, ascetical spirit and apostolate. At the time of his death, Opus Dei had more than 60,000 members from 80 different nationalities.

St Josemaría was a Consultor to the Pontifical Commission for the authentic interpretation of the Code of Canon Law, and to the Sacred Congregation for Seminaries and Universities. He was a Domestic Prelate and an honorary Academician of the Pontifical Roman Academy of Theology. He was also the Chancellor of the Universities of Navarre (in Spain) and Piura (in Peru).

St Josemaría died on 26 June 1975. For years, he had been offering his life for the Church and for the Pope. He was buried in the Crypt of the church of Our Lady of

Peace, in Rome. Blessed Alvaro del Portillo (1914-1994), who for many years had been his closest collaborator, was unanimously elected to succeed him. His successor in turn was Bishop Javier Echevarría (1932-2016), who had also worked for several decades with St Josemaría Escrivá and with Blessed Alvaro. Opus Dei, which from its inception had had the approval of the diocesan authorities and, from 1943, also the *appositio manuum* and subsequently the approval of the Holy See, was established as a Personal Prelature by His Holiness Pope John Paul II on 28 November 1982: this was the canonical formula foreseen and desired by St Josemaría Escrivá.

The reputation for holiness which the Founder of Opus Dei enjoyed in his life-time has spread after his death to the far corners of the earth, as can be seen from countless spiritual and material favours attributed to his intercession; among them, a number of cures which are medically in-explicable. Many letters from all the continents, and among them those of 69 Cardinals and nearly 1,300 Bishops (more than a third of the episcopate worldwide), were written requesting the Pope to open the Cause of Beatification and Canonisation of St Josemaría. The Congregation for the Causes of Saints gave its *nihil obstat* for the opening of the Cause on 30 January 1981 and this was ratified by Pope John Paul II on 5 February 1981.

Between 1981 and 1986 two processes took place, one in Rome and the other in Madrid, to gather information on the life and virtues of Msgr. Escrivá. Following the results of these two processes and accepting the favourable opinions of the congress of theological consultors and the Commission of Cardinals and Bishops members of the Congregation for the Causes of Saints, the Holy Father on 9 April 1990 declared the heroicity of the virtues of Msgr. Escrivá, who thus received the title of Venerable. On 6 July 1991 the Pope commanded the publication of a Decree declaring the miraculous nature of a cure attributed to the intercession of the Venerable Josemaría Escrivá. This act completed the juridical stages for the beatification of the Founder of Opus Dei, which was celebrated in Rome on 17 May 1992, in a solemn ceremony presided over by His Holiness Pope John Paul II in St Peter's Square. From 21 May 1992 the body of St Josemaría rests beneath the altar of the prelatic church of Our Lady of Peace, in the central offices of the Prelature of Opus Dei. It is accompanied constantly by the prayers and thanksgiving of many people from all over the world who have been brought closer to God, attracted by the example and teachings of the Founder of Opus Dei and by the devotion of those who turn to his intercession. Josemaría Escrivá was canonised in Rome on 6 October 2002.

Among his published writings, apart from the theological and legal study *La Abadesa de la Huelgas*, there are books of spirituality which have been translated into numerous languages: *The Way, Holy Rosary, Christ is passing by, Friends of God, The Way of the Cross, In Love with the Church, The Forge,* and *The Forge* (the last five titles have been published posthumously). Another book, which brings together press interviews, has the title *Conversations with Msgr. Escrivá de Balaguer*.

Preface

On 7 August 1931, the day the diocese of Madrid celebrated the Feast of the Transfiguration of Our Lord, Monsignor Escrivá made a note of a mystical experience granted to him by God. While he was saying Holy Mass that day, God gave him to understand in a new way the words of the Gospel, *et ego, si exaltatus fuero a terra, omnia traham ad meipsum.*[1] "I understood that it would be men and women of God who would raise the Cross with the doctrines of Christ on the summit of all human

[1] "Yes, if only I am lifted up from the earth, I will draw all things to myself" (John 12:32). This is how the sacred text then stood in the official Vulgate version.

activities ... And I saw the Lord triumph, drawing all things to himself." Then, as if in response to those lights, he continued: "In spite of feeling myself devoid of all virtue and knowledge (humility is the truth – this is no sham), I would like to write books of fire, which would run like wild-fire throughout the world, giving light and warmth to men, turning their poor hearts into burning coals, that can be offered to Jesus as rubies for his kingly crown."[2]

Those desires of his found expression in books like *The Way*, *Furrow*, and *The Forge*. Although *Furrow* and *The Forge* have been published posthumously, they were begun then, and I cannot imagine a more suitable description of them than the words of the author which I have just quoted. *The Forge* is a book of fire. Reading it and meditating on it can bring many souls to the forge of divine Love and enkindle within them a zeal for holiness and apostolate. That was the desire of Monsignor Escrivá, as is clearly reflected in the *Preface*: "How can I fail to

---

[2] J. Escrivá, 7 August 1931; manuscript notes kept in the Archive of the Prelature of the Holy Cross and Opus Dei.

take up your soul – pure gold – and place it in *the forge*, and fashion it with fire and hammer, until that gold nugget is turned into a splendid jewel to be offered to my God, to your God?"

The Forge contains 1055 points for meditation, arranged in thirteen chapters. Many of the points are clearly autobiographical. They come from notes written by the founder of Opus Dei in some spiritual copybooks, not exactly a diary, which he kept in the 1930s. In these personal jottings, he recorded incidents that showed the action of God in his soul, so that he could go over them and meditate on them in his personal prayer. He also recorded events and anecdotes from everyday life from which he always tried to draw some supernatural lesson. Monsignor Escrivá never liked drawing attention to himself, and so references to circumstances and events of an autobiographical nature are normally related in the third person.

Those of us who had the good fortune to be living by his side often heard him refer to this book, which had been taking shape gradually over the years. Apart from putting the book into its finished order, he had intended to read over each point carefully, so as to put all his priestly love at the service of his readers. He was not interested in *embellishing* these points. What he wanted was to enter into the intimate world of each person and while he waited for a suitable occasion to carry out this task ... God himself called him into His own intimacy. These words are now published exactly as their author left them.

The central theme of *The Forge* can be summarised in these words: "If we are faithful to him, Jesus' own life will somehow be repeated in the life of each one of us, both in its internal development (the process of sanctification) and in our outward behaviour" (418).

The progressive identification of the soul with Jesus Christ, which is the essence of the Christian life, is carried out in a hidden way through the Sacraments.[3] It also needs an effort from each one to correspond to grace: to know and love Our Lord, and

---

[3] cf. Second Vatican Council, Dogmatic Constitution, *Lumen gentium*, 7.

to have the same dispositions as he had.[4] The aim is to reproduce his life in our daily conduct, until we can exclaim with the Apostle: *Vivo autem, iam non ego: vivit vero in me Christus*,[5] it is not I who live, it is Christ who lives in me. God's programme for us – holiness – is thus explained to us. It is something which God asks of each of us without exception. "Just think, there are so many men and women on earth, and the Master does not fail to call every single one. He calls them to a Christian life, to a life of holiness, to a chosen life, to life eternal" (13).

This interior journey leading gradually to our identification with Christ is, as it were, the back-drop of *The Forge*. The book does not offer a rigid mould for the interior life. Nothing could be further from the intention of Monsignor Escrivá, who had the greatest respect for every person's interior freedom. For in the last analysis, each individual soul follows his own way under the guidance of the Holy Spirit. These points for meditation are in the

---

[4] cf. Phil 2:5

[5] Gal 2:20

nature of friendly suggestions, fatherly advice for souls who decide to take their Christian vocation seriously.

The Forge, as we shall see, follows the soul in its journey towards holiness, from the moment it perceives the light of a Christian vocation to the point when this earthly life opens out to eternity. The first chapter is about this very matter of vocation. The author called it *Dazzled*, because we are dazzled each time God makes us realise that we are his children, that we have cost the Blood, every drop of it, of his only-begotten Son and that – in spite of our nothingness and of our personal wretchedness – he wants us to be co-redeemers with Christ. "We are children of God, bearers of the only flame that can light up the paths of the earth for souls, of the only brightness which can never be darkened, dimmed or overshadowed" (1).

Responding to our divine vocation demands a constant warfare. Our fight is not a noisy one as it takes place on the battlefield of our ordinary life, for to be "a saint (...) doesn't mean doing strange things. It means a daily struggle in the interior life and in heroically fulfilling your duty right through to the end" (60).

We must accept that there will be defeats in this interior fight, and we may be threatened with the danger of discouragement. That is why the founder of Opus Dei constantly instilled in souls that cry of *possumus!* – "We can!" – of the sons of Zebedee.[6] It is not a cry that arises from presumption but from a humble trust in God's Omnipotence.

Monsignor Escrivá loved to use the example of the donkey. It is not a very handsome animal, but a humble and hard-working one, which earned the honour of bearing Jesus Christ in triumph through the streets of Jerusalem. The example of a persevering and obedient donkey, aware of its unworthiness, leads the author to encourage his readers to acquire and practise a series of virtues which, with his keen powers of observation, he discovered in the donkey which pulls the water-wheel. "Donkeys are humble, hard-working, persevering – stubborn – and faithful, with a sure step, tough and – if they have a good master – also grateful and

[6] Mark 10:39

obedient" (380).

Obedience is closely linked, in fact, with the humble perseverance of the little donkey at the water-wheel. "Be convinced that if you do not learn to obey you will never be effective" (626). For to obey the person who directs our soul and channels our apostolate in God's name, is to open ourselves to divine grace, and to let the Holy Spirit act in us. This requires humility. It is God, then, whom we obey. And the Church too, for God's sake. There is no other way: "Convince yourself, my child, that lack of unity within the Church is death" (631). This is another of those *basic ideas* in Monsignor Escrivá's preaching: not to separate Christ from his Church, nor to separate the Christian from Christ, to whom he is united by grace. Only thus will victory be assured.

Men and women who seek sanctity in the world carry out their apostolic tasks in, and by means of, the fulfilment of their ordinary duties. The first of these will be their job or profession. "From Saint Paul's teaching we know we have to renew the world in the spirit of Jesus Christ, that we have to place Our Lord at the summit and at the heart of all things. Do you think you are carrying this out in your work, in your professional task?" (678).

Together with work, all the other noble endeavours of men need to be converted into instruments of personal sanctity and apostolate. "You should be full of wonder at the goodness of Our Father God. Are you not filled with joy to know that your home, your family, your country, which you love so much, are the raw material which you must sanctify?" (689). And so, a number of points make reference to marriage and the family, and to our civic duties, for "the Lord wants his children, those of us who have received the gift of faith, to proclaim the original optimistic view of creation, the *love for the world* which is at the heart of the Christian message" (703).

The author often reminds us that we need a deep interior life if we are to "divinise things human"; otherwise we would run the risk of "humanising things divine". Nor should we forget – as I often heard Monsignor Escrivá say – that "every supernatural thing, when it refers to men, is also very human". That is why, the more complete one's identification with Christ becomes, the more pressing does apostolic zeal become, for, "whenever sanctity is genuine it overflows from its vessel to fill other hearts, other souls, with its superabundance" (856).

The Christian ends up acquiring a big heart, like Christ's, in which there is room for everybody. "Jesus will enable you to have a great affection for everybody you meet, without taking away any of the affection you have for him. On the contrary, the more you love Jesus, the more room there will be for other people in your heart" (876). And so, we come to detest any type of narrow-mindedness, any form of provincialism or exclusivism. Two attitudes typical of a mature soul are thus intertwined: an insatiable thirst for souls – "not a single soul – not one – can be a matter of indifference to you" (951) – and the equally insatiable desire to be united to God (cf 927).

Hunger for God can never be satisfied in this world, and so we seek complete union in *eternity*. This is the theme of the last chapter of *The Forge*. In the manner of Saint Paul, and in an especially intense way in the last years of his life, the Founder of Opus Dei felt both the desire of embracing his Love in Heaven as soon as possible (how often he repeated those words of the psalm: *vultum tuum, Domine, requiram!*[7]), and the desire to serve God effectively and for many years upon this earth. "To die is a good thing. How can anyone with faith be, at the same time, afraid to die? But as long as the Lord wants to keep you here on earth, it would be cowardice for you to want to die. You must live, live and suffer and work for Love: that is your task" (1037).

Thus there is a perfect continuity in the lives of the children of God: "Happiness in Heaven is for those who know how to be happy on earth" (1005). Happiness is the reward Jesus Christ promised his followers:[8] to be happy here, with a relative happiness, and to rejoice fully hereafter in the eternal life.

I venture to assure you, my dear reader, that if you and I enter into this *forge* of the Love of God, our souls will become better, being cleansed of some of the dross that

---

7 "Lord, I long to see thy face." (Ps 26:8)

8 cf. Matt 19:29

clings to them. Monsignor Escrivá will guide us along the ways of the interior life, with the firm steps of one who knows every inch of the terrain, having walked over it so many times. If we really do embark on this road, beginning and beginning again as often as necessary (cf. 384), we too shall reach the end of our journey full of peace and happiness, assured of a welcome in the arms of our Heavenly Father.

And do not forget that we are under Our Lady's protection. Let us turn to her as these pages end, with words from *The Forge*, so that by reading and meditating on this book we may obtain, by God's grace, the goal Monsignor Escrivá had in view for us when he wrote it. "Mother, do not leave me! Let me seek your Son, let me find your Son, let me love your Son – with my whole being" (157).

Alvaro del Portillo
Rome, 26 December 1986

Foreword

There was a mother
who, like all mothers,
was passionately fond of her little child,
whom she called
her prince, her king,
her treasure, her very sun.
I thought of you.
And I understood
– for what father does not carry
deep inside some maternal feelings? –
that it was no exaggeration
for that good mother to say:
you are more than a treasure,
you are worth more than the sun itself:
you are worth all Christ's Blood!
How can I fail to take up your soul
– pure gold –
and place it in the forge,
and fashion it with fire and hammer,
until that gold nugget is turned
into a splendid jewel
to be offered to my God,
to your God?

DAZZLED

1 We are children of God. –Bearers of the only flame that can light up the paths of the earth for souls, of the only brightness which can never be darkened, dimmed or overshadowed.

–The Lord uses us as torches, to make that light shine out... It depends on us that many should not remain in darkness, but walk instead along paths that lead to eternal life.

2 –God is my Father! If you meditate on it, you will never let go of this consoling consideration.

–Jesus is my intimate Friend (another re-discovery) who loves me with all the divine madness of his Heart.

–The Holy Spirit is my Consoler, who

guides my every step along the road.

Consider this often: you are God's… and God is yours.

3 My Father – talk to him like that, confidently – who art in heaven, look upon me with compassionate Love, and make me respond to thy love.

–Melt and enkindle my heart of bronze, burn and purify my unmortified flesh, fill my mind with supernatural light, make my tongue proclaim the Love and Glory of Christ.

4 Christ, who went up to the Cross with his arms wide open, with the gesture of the Eternal Priest, wants to count on us – who are nothing! – to bring to *all* men the fruits of his Redemption.

5 Lord, we are glad to find ourselves in your wounded palm. Grasp us tight, squeeze us hard, make us lose all our earthly wretchedness, purify us, set us on fire, make us feel drenched in your Blood.

–And then, cast us far, far away, hungry for the harvest, to sow the seed more fruitfully each day, for Love of you.

6 Do not be afraid. Do not be alarmed or surprised. Do not allow yourself to be overcome by false prudence.

The call to fulfil God's will – this goes for vocation too – is sudden, as it was for the Apostles: a meeting with Christ and his call is followed…

–None of them doubted. Meeting Christ and following him was all one.

7 A day of salvation, of eternity, has come for us. Once again the call of the Divine Shepherd can be heard, those affectionate words: *Vocavi te nomine tuo* – I have called you by your name.

Just like our mother, he calls us by our name, even by the name we were affectionately called at home. –There, in the depths of our soul, he calls us and we just have to answer: *Ecce ego quia vocasti me* –here I am, for you have called me, and this time I'm determined not to let time flow by like water over rounded stones, leaving no trace behind.

8 Live close to Christ! You should be another character in the Gospel, side by side with Peter, and John, and Andrew. For Christ is also living now: *Iesus Christus, heri et hodie, ipse et in saecula!* – Jesus Christ lives! Today, as yesterday, he is the same, for ever and ever.

9 Lord, may your children be like very well lit embers, showing no flames that would make the fire be seen from afar. Let them be embers that will set the first light on each heart they come into contact with.

–You will make that first spark turn into a big fire, because your Angels are very skilled at blowing on embers in hearts... I know, I have seen it. And a heart cleared of dead ashes cannot but be yours.

10 Think about what the Holy Spirit says, and let yourself be filled with awe and gratitude: *Elegit nos ante mundi constitutionem* – he chose us before the foundation of the world, *ut essemus sancti in conspectu eius!* – that we might be holy in his presence.

–To be holy isn't easy, but it isn't

difficult either. To be holy is to be a good Christian, to resemble Christ. The more closely a person resembles Christ, the more Christian he is, the more he belongs to Christ, the holier he is.

–And what means do we have? The same means the early faithful had, when they saw Jesus directly or caught a glimpse of him in the accounts the Apostles and Evangelists gave of him.

11 You owe such a great debt to your Father-God! He has given you life, intelligence, will... He has given you his grace: the Holy Spirit; Jesus, in the Sacred Host; divine sonship; the Blessed Virgin, the Mother of God and our Mother. He has given you the possibility of taking part in the Holy Mass; and he grants you forgiveness for your sins. He forgives you so many times! He has given you countless gifts, some of them quite extraordinary...

Tell me, my son: how have you corresponded so far to this generosity? How are you corresponding now?

12 I do not know how it strikes you…,

but I feel I must tell you how moved I am whenever I read the words of the prophet Isaiah: *Ego vocavi te nomine tuo, meus es tu!* – I have called you, I have brought you into my Church, you are mine! God himself telling me I am his! It is enough to make one go mad with Love!

13 Just think, there are so many men and women on earth, and the Master does not fail to call every single one.

He calls them to a Christian life, to a life of holiness, to a chosen life, to life eternal.

14 Christ suffered in your place and for your benefit, to tear you away from the slavery of sin and imperfection.

15 In these times of violence and of brutal, savage sexuality, we have to be rebels: we refuse point blank to go with the tide, and become beasts.

We want to behave like children of God, like men and women who are on intimate terms with their Father, who is in Heaven and who wants to be very close to – inside! – each one of us.

16 Meditate on this frequently: I am a Catholic, a child of Christ's Church. He brought me to birth in a home that is *his*, without my doing anything to deserve it.

–My God, how much I owe you.

17 Remind everyone (and especially all those fathers and mothers, who call themselves Christians) that a *vocation*, a call from God, is a grace from the Lord, a choice made by the divine goodness, a reason for holy pride, a call to serve all joyously for the love of Jesus Christ.

18 Please echo these words for me: it is no "sacrifice" for parents when God asks them for their children. Neither, for those he calls, is it a sacrifice to follow him.

It is, on the contrary, an immense honour, a reason for a great and holy pride, a mark of predilection, a very special affection that God has shown at a particular time, but which has been in his mind from all eternity.

19 Be grateful to your parents for bringing you into this world, thus enabling you to become a child of God. And be all the more grateful if it was they who placed in your soul the first seeds of faith and piety, of your Christian way, or of your vocation.

20 There are many people around you, and you have no right to be an obstacle to their spiritual good, to their eternal happiness.

–You are under an obligation to be a saint. You must not let God down for having chosen you. Neither must you let those around you down: they expect so much from your Christian life.

21 The commandment to love our parents belongs to both natural law and to divine positive law, and I have always called it a "most sweet precept".

–Do not neglect your obligation to love your parents more each day, to mortify yourself for them, to pray for them and to be grateful to them for all the good you owe them.

22 Following the Master's wishes, you are to be salt and light while being fully immersed in this world we were made to live in, sharing in all human activities. Light which illuminates the hearts and minds of men. Salt which gives flavour and preserves from corruption.

That is why if you lack apostolic zeal you will become insipid and useless. You will be letting other people down and your life will be absurd.

23 A red and blue wave of filth and corruption has set out to overcome the world, throwing its vile spittle over the Cross of the Redeemer.

Now He wants another wave to issue out from our souls – a wave that's white and powerful, like the Lord's right hand – to overcome with its purity all the rottenness of materialism and undo the corruption that has flooded the world. It is for this, and more, that the children of God have come.

24 Many people ask with an air of self-justification: Why should I get involved in the lives of others?

–Because it is your Christian duty to get involved in their lives, in order to serve them!

–Because Christ has got involved in your life and in mine!

25 If you are another Christ, if you behave as a son of God, wherever you are you will set others alight. Christ burns with love, he does not leave hearts indifferent.

26 It is painful to see that after two thousand years there are so few people in the world who call themselves Christians and that of those who do call themselves Christians, so few practise the true teaching of Jesus Christ.

It is worth while putting our whole life at stake!: working and suffering for Love, to accomplish God's plans and co-redeem.

27 I look at your Cross, my Jesus, and I rejoice in your grace, because your Calvary has won for us the reward of the Holy Spirit. And you give yourself to me, each day, lovingly, *madly*, in the Sacred Host. And you have made me *a son of God*, and have given me your Mother to be mine.

I can't be satisfied with just giving thanks. My thoughts take flight: Lord, Lord, there are so many souls who are so far from you!

Foster those yearnings for apostolate in your life, that many may get to know him…, and love him…, and come to feel loved by him!

28 Sometimes we hear love described (you'll have heard me mention this more than once) as if it were a movement towards self-satisfaction, or merely a means of selfishly fulfilling one's own personality.

–And I have always told you that it isn't so. True love demands getting out of oneself, giving oneself. Genuine love brings joy in its wake, a joy that has its roots in the shape of the Cross.

29 My God, how is it that I do not cry out in sorrow and love whenever I see a Crucifix?

30 Marvel at God's magnanimity: he has become Man to redeem us, so that you and I – who are absolutely worthless, admit it! – may come to know him and trust him.

31 O Jesus…, strengthen our souls, open out the way for us, and, above all, intoxicate us with your Love! Make us into blazing fires to kindle the earth with the heavenly fire you brought us.

32 Coming closer to God means being ready to be converted anew, to change direction again, to listen attentively to his inspirations – those holy desires he places in our souls – and to put them into practice.

33 What are you so proud of? – Every impulse that moves you comes from Him. Act accordingly.

34 What respect, veneration and affection we should feel for every single soul when we realise that God loves it as his very own!

35 An aspiration: May we spend the days the Lord grants us only in pleasing him!

36 I would like you to behave as Peter and John did – speaking to Jesus about the needs of your friends, colleagues… as you pray. And then with your example you will be able to say to them: *Respice in nos!* – look at me!.

37 When you love somebody very much, you want to know everything about him.

–Meditate on this: Do you feel a hunger to know Christ? Because… that is the measure of your love for him.

38 People who say that we priests are lonely are either lying or have got it all wrong. We are far less lonely than anyone else, for we can count on the constant company of the Lord, with whom we should be conversing without interruption.

–We are in love with Love, with the Author of Love!

39 I see myself like a poor little bird, accustomed only to making short flights from tree to tree, or, at most, up to a third floor balcony… One day in its life it succeeded in reaching the roof of a modest building, that you could hardly call a skyscraper.

But suddenly our little bird is snatched up by an eagle, who mistakes the bird for one of its own brood. In its powerful talons the bird is borne higher and higher, above the mountains of the earth and the snow-capped peaks, above the white, blue and rose-pink clouds, and higher and higher until it can look right into the sun. And then the eagle lets go of the little bird and says: Off you go. Fly!

–Lord, may I never flutter again close to the ground. May I always be enlightened by the rays of the divine sun – Christ – in the Eucharist. May my flight never be interrupted until I find repose in your Heart.

40 That friend of ours would finish his prayer in this way: "I love the Will of my God and that is why, abandoning myself completely into his hands, I pray that he may lead me however and wherever he likes."

41 Ask the Father, the Son and the Holy Spirit, and your Mother, to make you know yourself and weep for all those foul things that have passed through you, and which, alas, have left such dregs behind... – And at the same time, without wishing to stop considering all that, say to him: Jesus, give me a Love that will act like a purifying fire in which my miserable flesh, my miserable heart, my miserable soul, my miserable body may be consumed and cleansed of all earthly wretchedness. And when I have been completely emptied of myself, fill me with yourself. May I never become attached to anything here below. May Love always sustain me.

42 Desire nothing for yourself, either good or bad. For yourself, want only what God wants.

Whatever it may be, if it comes from his hand, from God, however bad it may appear in the eyes of men, with God's help it will appear good, yes very good!, to you. And with an ever-increasing conviction you will say: *Et in tribulatione mea dilatasti me... et calix tuus inebrians, quam praeclarus est!* – I have rejoiced in tribulation..., how marvellous is your chalice. It inebriates my whole being!

43 We should offer the Lord the

sacrifice of Abel. A sacrifice of lovely young flesh, the best of the flock; of healthy and holy flesh; a sacrifice of hearts that have one love alone – you, my God. A sacrifice of minds, which have been shaped through deep study and will surrender to your Wisdom; of childlike souls who will think only of pleasing you.

–Lord, receive even now this sweet and fragrant sacrifice.

44 We have to learn how to give ourselves, to burn before God like the light placed on a lampstand to give light to those who walk in darkness; like the sanctuary lamps that burn by the altar, giving off light till they are consumed.

45 The Lord, the teacher of Love, is a jealous lover who asks for all we possess, for all our love. He expects us to offer him whatever we have, and to follow the path he has marked out for each one of us.

46 My God, I see I shall never accept you as my Saviour unless I acknowledge you as my Model at the same time.

–Since you yourself chose to be poor, make me love holy poverty. I resolve, with your grace, to live and die in poverty, even though I may have millions at my disposal.

47 You became very thoughtful when I told you: "The way I see it, everything seems too little when it is for the Lord."

48 It would be good if it could be said of you that the distinguishing feature of your life was "loving God's Will".

49 Any job, no matter how hidden, no matter how insignificant, when offered to the Lord, is charged with the strength of God's life!

50 Feel the responsibility of your mission: the whole of Heaven is looking down on you.

51 God awaits you! – So, wherever you are, you must commit yourself to imitating him and uniting yourself to him, cheerfully, lovingly, keenly, though circumstances might require you – even permanently – to go against the grain.

God awaits you!... and needs you to be faithful!

52 You wrote: "My King, I hear you proclaiming in a loud voice that still resounds: *Ignem veni mittere in terram, et quid volo nisi ut accendatur?* – I have come to cast fire upon the earth, and would that it were already kindled!"

Then you added: "Lord, it is me – all of me – who answers with all my senses and faculties: *Ecce ego quia vocasti me!* – here I am because you have called me."

–May this answer of yours be a daily reality.

53 You should show the moderation, fortitude and sense of responsibility that many people acquire after many long years, in their old age. You will achieve all this, while you are still young, if you do not – I beg you – lose the supernatural outlook of a son of God. For he will give you, more than to the old, those qualities you need for your apostle's work.

54 You enjoy an interior happiness and

peace that you would not exchange for anything in the world. God is here. There is no better way than telling him our woes for them to cease being such.

55 Is it possible, you asked me, that Christ should have spent so many years – twenty centuries – acting on earth, and the world should be now what it is? Is it possible, you went on, that there should still be people who do not know Our Lord?

–And I answered you with conviction: It is our fault. For we have been called to be co-redeemers, and at times, perhaps often!, we do not follow the Will of God.

56 How humble Jesus is. What a shame, in contrast, that I who am nothing but dust from a dung-heap should so often have disguised my pride under the cloak of dignity, or justice. – And as a result, how many opportunities to follow the Master I have missed or wasted, by failing to supernaturalise them.

57 Sweet Mother..., lead us to that madness that will make others fall madly in love with our Christ.

Sweet Lady Mary, may Love not be in us a flash in the pan, or a will-o'-the-wisp, such as decomposing corpses sometimes produce. May it be a true devouring fire, which sets alight and burns everything it touches.

STRUGGLE

58 Being chosen by God means – and demands*!* – personal holiness.

59 If you respond to the call the Lord has made to you, your life – your poor life! – will leave a deep and wide furrow in the history of the human race, a clear and fertile furrow, eternal and godly.

60 Each day be conscious of your duty to be a saint. –A saint! And that doesn't mean doing strange things. It means a daily struggle in the interior life and in heroically fulfilling your duty right through to the end.

61 Sanctity does not consist in great

concerns. –It consists in struggling to ensure that the flame of your supernatural life is never allowed to go out; it consists in letting yourself to be burned down to the last shred, serving God in the lowest place... or in the highest: wherever the Lord may call you.

62 Our Lord did not confine himself to telling us that he loved us. He showed it us with deeds, with his whole life. –What about you?

63 If you love the Lord, you will *necessarily* feel the blessed burden of souls, and the need to bring them to God.

64 For someone who wants to live for Love with a capital letter, the middle course is not good enough; that would be meanness, a wretched compromise.

65 Here is a recipe for your way as a Christian: pray, do penance, work without rest, fulfilling your duty lovingly.

66 My God, teach me how to love! –My

God, teach me how to pray!

67 We must ask God for faith, hope and charity, with humility, with persevering prayer, with upright behaviour and a clean life.

68 You told me that you did not know how to repay me for the holy zeal that flooded your soul.

–I hastened to answer: It is not I who have given you any of those yearnings; it is the Holy Spirit.

–Desire his company, get to know him. –That way you will come to love him better and better, and you will come to thank him for taking up his abode in your soul so that you may have interior life.

69 Keep struggling, so that the Holy Sacrifice of the Altar really becomes the centre and the root of your interior life, and so your whole day will turn into an act of worship – an extension of the Mass you have attended and a preparation for the next. Your whole day will then be an act of worship that overflows in aspirations, visits to the Blessed Sacrament and the offering up of your professional work and your family life…

70 Try to give thanks to Jesus in the Eucharist by singing the praises of Our Lady, the Virgin most pure, without stain, who brought forth the Lord into this world.

–And, with childlike daring, say to Jesus: My dearest Love, blessed be the Mother who brought you into this world!

I assure you it will please him, and he will put even greater love in your soul.

71 Saint Luke the Evangelist tells us that Jesus prayed... What must his prayer have been like!

Contemplate this fact slowly: the disciples had the opportunity of talking to Jesus and in their conversations with him the Lord taught them by his words, and deeds, how they should pray. And he taught them this amazing truth of God's mercy: that we are God's children and that we can address Him as a child addresses his Father.

72 When you start out each day to work

by Christ's side and to look after all those souls who seek him, remember that there is only one way of doing it: we must turn to the Lord.

–Only in prayer, and through prayer, do we learn to serve others!

73 Remember that prayer does not consist in making pretty speeches, or high-sounding or consoling phrases.

Prayer, at times, will be a glance at a picture of Our Lord or of his Mother; sometimes a petition, expressed in words; or offering good works, and the fruits of faithfulness…

We have to be like a guard on sentry duty at the gate of God Our Lord: that's what prayer is. Or like a small dog that lies down at his master's feet.

–Do not mind telling him: Lord, here I am, like a faithful dog; or better still like a little donkey, which will not kick the one who loves him.

74 We all have to be *ipse Christus* – Christ himself. This is what Saint Paul commands in the name of God: *Induimini*

Dominum Iesum Christum – put on the Lord Jesus Christ.

Each one of us – you! – has to see how he puts on that clothing of which the Apostle speaks. Each one personally, has to sustain an uninterrupted dialogue with the Lord.

75 Your prayer cannot stop at mere words. It has to lead to deeds and practical consequences.

76 To pray is the way to keep all the evils we suffer in check.

77 Here is a piece of advice I shall never tire of telling souls: Love the Mother of God madly, for she is our Mother.

78 Heroism, sanctity, daring, require a constant spiritual preparation. You can only ever give to others what you already have. And, to give God to them, you yourself need to get to know him, to live his Life, to serve him.

79 I will not stop repeating until it is

deeply engraved in your soul: Piety, piety, piety! For if you lack charity it will be for want of interior life, not for any defect of character.

80 If you are a good son of God, in the same way that a little child needs to be assured of the presence of his parents when he gets up in the morning or goes to bed at night, your first and last thought each day will be for Him.

81 You must be constant and demanding with yourself in your regular practices of piety, also when you feel tired or they seem to be arid. Persevere! Those moments are like the tall red-painted poles which serve as markers along the mountain roads when there are heavy snowfalls. They are *always* there to show where it is safe to go.

82 Make an effort to respond at each moment to what God is asking of you: have the will to love him with deeds. –They may be little deeds, but don't leave out a single one.

83 Interior life is strengthened by a daily struggle in your practices of piety, which you should fulfil – or rather which you should live! – lovingly, because the path we travel as children of God is a path of Love.

84 Seek God in the depths of your pure, clean heart; in the depths of your soul when you are faithful to him. And never lose that intimacy.

–And if ever you do not know how to speak to him or what to say, or you do not dare to look for Jesus inside yourself, turn to Mary, *tota pulchra*, all pure and wonderful, and tell her: Our Lady and Mother, the Lord wanted you yourself to look after God and tend him with your own hands. Teach me, teach us all, how to treat your Son!

85 You must instil in all souls the heroism of doing the little things of each day perfectly, as if the salvation of the world depended on each one of those actions.

86 With your life of piety you will learn

how to practise the virtues proper to your condition as a son of God, as a Christian.

–And together with those virtues you will acquire a whole range of spiritual values which seem small but are really very great. They are like shining precious stones, and we must gather them along the way and then take them up to the foot of God's Throne in the service of our fellow men: simplicity, cheerfulness, loyalty, peace, small renunciations, services which pass unnoticed, the faithful fulfilment of duty, kindness…

87 Don't create more obligations for yourself than… God's glory, his Love, his Apostolate.

88 Our Lord has made you see your way clearly as a Christian in the middle of the world. Nevertheless, you tell me that you have often thought, enviously (though in the end you admitted it would be taking the easy way out) of the happiness of being a nobody, of working away, totally obscure, in the remotest corner… God and you!

–Now, apart from the idea of

missionary work in Japan, the thought of just such a hidden and sacrificed life has come to your mind. But if, free from other holy natural obligations, you were to try to "hide away" in a religious institution, assuming that was not your vocation, you would not be happy. You would lack peace; because you would have done your own will, not God's.

–Your "vocation", in that case, would deserve another name: it would be a defection. It would not be the result of divine inspiration, but of sheer human reluctance to face the coming struggle. And that would never do!

89 In living holy purity and a clean life, there is a great difficulty to which we are all exposed. The danger is one of becoming *bourgeois*, either in our spiritual life or in our professional life; the danger – also a real one for those called by God to marriage – of becoming dry old bachelors, selfish; people who do not love.

–Fight that danger tooth and nail, without making concessions of any kind.

90 Because we shall always have to put up with this little donkey which is our body, to conquer sensuality you have to practise daily and generously little mortifications – and sometimes big ones as well. And you must live in the presence of God, who never ceases to watch over you.

91 Your chastity cannot be confined to avoiding falls or occasions… In no way can it be a cold and mathematical negative.

–Haven't you realised that chastity is a *virtue* and that as such it should grow and become more perfect?

–It is not enough, then, to be continent according to your state. You have to be chaste, with a heroic virtue.

92 The *bonus odor Christi*, the fragrance of Christ, is also that of our clean life, of our chastity – the chastity of each one in his own state, I repeat – of our holy purity, which is a joyful affirmation. It is something solid and at the same time gentle; it is refined, avoiding even the use of inappropriate words, since they cannot be pleasing to God.

93 Get used to thanking the Guardian Angels in advance, thus putting them under an obligation.

94 One ought to be able to apply to every Christian the name that was used in the early ages: *Bearer of God.*

–Your actions should be such that you *really* deserve to be called by that wonderful name.

95 Think what would happen if we Christians chose not to behave as such... and then rectify your behaviour.

96 Discover Our Lord behind each event and in every circumstance, and then, from everything that happens, you will be able to draw more love for God and a greater desire to respond to him. He is always waiting for us, offering us the possibility to fulfil at all times that resolution we made: *Serviam!* I will serve you!

97 Renew each day the effective desire to empty yourself, to deny yourself, to forget yourself, to walk *in novitate sensus*, with a new life, exchanging this misery of ours for all the hidden and eternal grandeur of God.

98 Lord, make me so much yours that not even the holiest affections may enter my heart except through your wounded Heart.

99 Try to be considerate, well-mannered. Don't be boorish!

–Try to be polite always, which doesn't mean being affected.

100 Charity succeeds always. Without charity nothing can be done.

Love, then, is the secret of your life... Do love! Suffer gladly. Toughen up your soul. Invigorate your will. Make sure that you surrender yourself to God's will, and efficacy will follow.

101 Have the piety and simplicity of a child, and the strength and fortitude of a leader.

102 Peace, and the joy which comes with it, cannot be given by the world.

–Men are forever "making peace" and forever getting entangled in wars. This is because they have forgotten the advice to struggle inside themselves and to go to God for help. Then He will conquer, and we will obtain peace for ourselves and for our own homes, for society and for the world.

If we do things in this way, you and I will have joy, because it is the possession of those who conquer. And with the grace of God – who never loses battles – we will be able to count ourselves conquerors as long as we are humble.

103 Your life, your work, should never be negative, nor *anti* anything. It is – it must be! – positive, optimistic, youthful, cheerful and peaceful.

104 In national life there are two things which are really essential: the laws concerning marriage and the laws to do with education. In these areas the children of God have to stand firm and fight with toughness and fairness, for the sake of all mankind.

105 Joy is a Christian possession which

we will have as long as we keep fighting, for it is a consequence of peace. Peace is the fruit of having conquered in war, and the life of man upon this earth – as we read in Sacred Scripture – is a warfare.

106 This divine warfare of ours is a marvellous sowing of peace.

107 The person who stops struggling causes harm to the Church, to his own supernatural undertaking, to his brothers and to all souls.

–Examine yourself. Could you not put a more lively love for God into your spiritual combat? –I am praying for you… and for everyone. You should do the same.

108 Jesus, if there is anything in me which is displeasing to you, tell me what it is so that we may uproot it.

109 There is an enemy of the interior life which is both little and silly. Unfortunately, it can be very effective. It is the neglect of effort in one's examination of conscience.

110 In Christian asceticism the examination of conscience meets a need of love, and of sensitivity.

111 If there is anything in you that is out of harmony with God's spirit, get rid of it straight away!

Think of the Apostles. They were not of much account, yet they could work miracles in the name of the Lord. Only Judas, who at one time may also have worked miracles, went astray by voluntarily separating himself from Christ, because he did not cut himself away violently and courageously from what was out of harmony with God's spirit.

112 My God, when am I going to convert?

113 Don't wait until you are old to start becoming a saint. That would be a great mistake!

–Begin right now, in earnest, cheerfully and joyfully, by fulfilling the duties of your work and of your everyday life.

Don't wait until you are old to

become a saint. Because – I insist – apart from its being a great mistake, you never know whether you will live as long as that.

114 Ask the Lord to grant you all the sensitivity you need to realise how evil venial sin is, so as to recognise it as an outright and fundamental enemy of your soul, and, with God's grace, to avoid it.

115 Calmly, without scruples, you should think about your life, and ask forgiveness, and make a firm, specific and well-defined resolution to improve in one point and another: in that small detail which you find hard, and in that other one which usually you don't carry out as you should, and you know it.

116 Fill yourself with good desires, which is a holy thing, praised by God. But don't leave it at that! You have to be a soul – a man, a woman – who deals in realities. To carry out those good desires, you have to formulate clear and precise resolutions.

–And then, my child, you have to *fight* to put them into practice, with God's grace.

117 "What do I have to do to maintain my love for God and make it increase?" you asked me, fired with enthusiasm.

–Leave the "old man" behind, my son, and cheerfully give up things which are good in themselves but hinder your detachment from your ego... You have to repeat constantly and with deeds, "Here I am, Lord, ready to do whatever you want."

118 A saint! A son of God should exaggerate in practising virtue – if exaggeration is possible here... Because other people will see themselves reflected in him, as in a mirror, and it is only by our aiming very high that others will reach a middling level.

119 Don't be ashamed to discover in your heart the *fomes peccati* – the inclination to evil, which will be with you as long as you live, for nobody is free from this burden.

Don't be ashamed, because the all-powerful and merciful Lord has given us all the means we need for overcoming this inclination: the Sacraments, a life of piety and sanctified work.

–Persevere in using these means, ever ready to begin again and again without getting discouraged.

120 Lord, rescue me from myself!

121 An apostle who does not pray regularly and methodically will necessarily fall into lukewarmness... and he will then cease to be an apostle.

122 Lord, from now on let me be another: no longer "me", but that "other person" you would like me to be.

–Let me not deny you anything you ask of me. Let me know how to pray. Let me know how to suffer. Let me not worry about anything except your glory. Let me feel your presence all the time.

–May I love the Father. May I hunger for you, my Jesus, in a permanent Communion. May the Holy Spirit set me on fire.

123 *Meus es tu* – you are mine, the Lord has declared to you.

–To think that God, who is all beauty

and all wisdom, all splendour and all goodness, should say to you that you are his...! and then, after all this, you can't bring yourself to respond to him!

124 You should not be surprised to feel in your life that weight dragging you down which Saint Paul spoke of: "I see in my members another law at war with the law of my mind."

–Remember then that you belong to Christ, and have recourse to the Mother of God, who is your Mother. They will not abandon you.

125 Receive the advice you are given in spiritual guidance as though it came from Jesus Christ himself.

126 You asked me to suggest a way for winning through in your daily struggles, and I replied: When you lay your soul open, say first of all what you wouldn't like to be known. In this way the devil will always end up defeated.

–Lay your soul wide open, clearly and simply, so that the rays of God's Love may reach and illuminate the last corner of it!

127 If that dumb devil mentioned in the Gospel gets into your soul, he will spoil everything. On the other hand, if you get rid of him immediately, everything will turn out well; you will carry on merrily, and all will be well.

–A firm resolution: to be "savagely sincere" in spiritual direction, always keeping your good manners…, and to be sincere immediately.

128 Love and seek help from the person who guides your soul. In spiritual direction lay your heart completely open – rotten, if it were rotten! – with all sincerity, with the desire to be cured. If you don't, you will never get rid of that rottenness.

If you go to someone who can only cleanse the wound superficially… you are a coward, because really you will be going along to hide the truth, doing yourself harm.

129 Never be afraid of telling the truth. But don't forget that sometimes it is better to remain silent out of charity towards your neighbour. However, you should never be silent out of laziness, or love of comfort, or cowardice.

130 The world thrives on lies even twenty centuries after the Truth came among men.

–We have to tell the truth! This is precisely what we have to do as children of God. When men get used to proclaiming and hearing the truth, there will be more understanding in this world of ours.

131 It would be a false charity, a diabolical, deceitful charity, to give way in matters of faith. We must be *fortes in fide* – strong in faith, firm, as Saint Peter demands.

–This is not fanaticism, but quite simply the practice of our faith. It does not entail disliking anyone. We can give way in all accidental matters, but in matters of faith we cannot give way. We cannot spare the oil from our lamps, otherwise when the Bridegroom comes he will find they have burned out.

132 Humility and obedience are the

indispensable conditions for acquiring good doctrine.

133 Welcome the Pope's words with a religious, humble, internal and effective acceptance. And pass them on!

134 You must love, venerate, pray and mortify yourself for the Pope, and do so with greater affection each day. He is the foundation stone of the Church and, throughout the centuries, right to the end of time, he carries out among men that task of sanctifying and governing which Jesus entrusted to Peter.

135 Your deepest love, your greatest esteem, your most heartfelt veneration, your most complete obedience and your warmest affection have also to be shown towards the Vicar of Christ on earth, towards the Pope.

We Catholics should consider that after God and the most Holy Virgin, our Mother, the Holy Father comes next in the hierarchy of love and authority.

136 May the daily consideration of the heavy burden which weighs on the Pope and the bishops move you to venerate and love them with real affection, and to help them with your prayers.

137 Your love for Our Lady should be more lively, more supernatural.

–Don't just go to the Virgin Mary to ask her for things. You should also go to give!: give her your affection; give her your love for her divine Son; and show her your affection with deeds of service to others, who are also her children.

138 Jesus is our model. Let us imitate him.

Let us imitate him by serving the Holy Church and all mankind.

139 When contemplating the scene of the Incarnation, strengthen in your soul the resolve to be "humble in practice". See how he lowered himself, taking on our poor nature.

–That is why every day you need to react, right away, with God's grace, accepting – and wanting – the humiliations the Lord may offer you.

140 Live your Christian life with naturalness! Let me stress this: make Christ known through your behaviour, just as an ordinary mirror reproduces an image without distorting it or turning it into a caricature. – If, like the mirror, you are *normal*, you will reflect Christ's life, and show it to others.

141 If you are fatuous, if all you can think of is your own personal comfort, if you centre everyone else and even the world itself on yourself, then you have no right to call yourself a Christian or to consider yourself a disciple of Christ. He set the level of what can be demanded of us when he offered, for each of us: *et animam suam*, his own soul, his whole life.

142 Try to make "intellectual humility" an axiom in your life.

Think about it carefully… Isn't it true that it just doesn't make sense to be "intellectually proud"? That saint and doctor of the Church put it very well when he said: "It is a detestable disorder for a man to see God become a little child, and yet still want to appear great in this world."

143 The moment you have anyone – whoever he may be – at your side, find a way, without doing anything strange, to pass on to him the joy you experience in being a son of God and living as such.

144 The mission to serve which the Divine Master has entrusted to us is a great and beautiful mission. –That is why this good spirit – which entails great self-mastery! – is perfectly compatible with the love of freedom that should pervade the work of all Christians.

145 You must never treat anyone unmercifully. If you think someone is not worthy of your mercy, you should realise that neither do you deserve anything.

–You don't deserve to have been created, or to be a Christian, or to be a son of God, or to have the family you have...

146 Don't neglect the practice of fraternal correction, which is a clear sign of the supernatural virtue of charity. It's hard;

because it's easier to be inhibited. Easier!, but not supernatural.

–And for such omissions you will have to render an account to God.

147 When you have to make a fraternal correction, do it with great kindness – great charity! – in what you say and in the way you say it, for at that moment you are God's instrument.

148 If you know how to love other people and you spread that affection – Christ's kindly, gentle charity – all around you, you will be able to support one another, and if someone is about to stumble he will feel that he is being supported, and also encouraged, to be faithful to God through this fraternal strength.

149 Bring out your spirit of mortification in those nice touches of charity, eager to make the way of sanctity in the middle of the world attractive for everyone. Sometimes a smile can be the best proof of a spirit of penance.

150 May you know how to put yourself out cheerfully, discreetly and generously each day, serving others and making their lives more pleasant.

–To act in this way is the true charity of Jesus Christ.

151 You should make sure that wherever you are there is that *good humour* – that cheerfulness – which is born of an interior life.

152 Make sure you practise this very interesting mortification: that of not making your conversation revolve around yourself.

153 Here is a good way of doing an examination of conscience:

–Have I accepted in a spirit of expiation the difficulties which have come to me this day from the hand of God? Or those which came from the behaviour of my colleagues? Or from my own wretchedness?

–Have I managed to offer Our Lord, in expiation, the very sorrow I feel for having offended him *so many times*? Have

I offered him the shame of all my inner embarrassment and humiliation at seeing how little progress I make along the path of virtue?

154 Habitual and customary mortifications are a good thing, but don't become one-track minded about them.

–They need not necessarily be the same ones all the time. What should be constant, habitual and customary – without your getting accustomed to it – is to have a spirit of mortification.

155 You want to follow in Christ's footsteps, to wear his livery, to identify yourself with Jesus. Well then, make your faith a living faith, full of sacrifice and deeds of service, and get rid of everything that stands in the way.

156 Sanctity has the flexibility of supple muscles. Whoever wishes to be a saint should know how to behave so that while he does something that involves a mortification for him, he omits doing something else – as long as this does not offend God – which he would also find difficult, and thanks the Lord for this comfort. If we Christians were to act otherwise we would run the risk of becoming stiff and lifeless, like a rag doll.

Sanctity is not rigid like cardboard; it knows how to smile, to give way to others and to hope. It is life – a supernatural life.

157 Mother, do not leave me! Let me seek your Son, let me find your Son, let me love your Son – with my whole being! –Remember me, my Lady, remember me.

DEFEAT

158 When our vision is clouded, when our eyes have lost their clarity, we need to go to the light. And Jesus Christ has told us that he is the Light of the world and that he has come to heal the sick.

–That is why, your weaknesses and your falls – when God allows them – should not separate you from Christ, but rather draw you closer to him!

159 In my wretchedness I complained to a friend of mine, saying that it seemed as if Jesus were passing me by… and leaving me on my own.

–But immediately I thought better of it and was sorry. Full of confidence, I said: It is not true, my Love. Quite clearly it is I who have gone away from you. Never again!

160 Beg the Lord for his grace so that you may be purified by his Love… and by constant penance.

161 Turn to Our Lady and ask her – as a token of her love for you – for the gift of contrition. Ask that you may be sorry, with the sorrow of Love, for all your sins and for the sins of all men and women throughout the ages.

And with that same disposition, be bold enough to add: "Mother, my life, my hope, lead me by the hand… And if there is anything in me which is displeasing to my Father God grant that I may see it, so that, between the two of us, we may uproot it."

Do not be afraid to continue: "O clement, O loving, O sweet Virgin Mary, pray for me, that by fulfilling the most lovable Will of your Son, I may be worthy to obtain and enjoy what Our Lord Jesus has promised."

162 Heavenly Mother, let me regain

once more fervour, dedication, self-denial: in one word, Love.

163 You shouldn't be so easy on yourself! Don't wait until the New Year to make your resolutions. Every day is a good day to make good decisions. *Hodie, nunc!* – Today, now!

It tends to be the poor defeatist types who leave it until the New Year before beginning afresh… And even then, they never really begin.

164 I agree. You acted badly, out of weakness. –But what I fail to understand is how, with a clear conscience, you have not repented. You cannot do something wrong and then say, or think, that it is something holy, or that it is of no importance.

165 You must always remember that the spiritual faculties are fed by what they receive from the senses. Guard them well!

166 As you very well know, you lose your peace when you consent in matters which entail unfaithfulness to your way.

–Make up your mind to be consistent and responsible in your behaviour!

167 The indelible memory of the favours you have received from God should always be a compelling force within you; especially so in times of tribulation.

168 There is but one fatal illness, one deadly mistake you can make: to settle for defeat, not to know how to fight with the spirit of a child of God. If this personal effort is lacking, the soul becomes paralysed and languishes alone, and is incapable of bearing fruit.

–Such cowardice on man's part puts pressure on Our Lord to utter those words addressed to him by the paralytic at the pool of Bethsaida, *hominem non habeo!* – I have no man to help me.

–What a pity if Jesus does not find in you the man or the woman he expects!

169 The ascetical struggle is not something negative and therefore hateful, but rather a joyful affirmation. It is a sport.

A good sportsman doesn't fight to

gain just one victory, and that at the first attempt. He has to build himself up for it, training over a long period of time, calmly and confidently. He keeps trying again and again, and if he doesn't succeed at the first attempt, he keeps on trying with determination until the obstacle is overcome.

170 You are my hope in all things, dear Jesus. Convert me!

171 When that priest, our good friend, used to sign himself "the sinner", he did so convinced that what he wrote was true.

–My God, purify me too!

172 If you have done something wrong, be it big or small, go running back to God!

–Savour those words of the psalm, *cor contritum et humiliatum, Deus, non despicies* – the Lord will never spurn or disregard a contrite and humbled heart.

173 Keep turning this over in your mind and in your soul: Lord, how many times you have lifted me up when I have fallen and once my sins have been forgiven have held me close to your Heart!

Keep returning to the thought... and never separate yourself from Him again.

174 You see yourself as a poor man whose master has stripped him of his livery. You are only a sinner! And you understand the nakedness felt by our first parents.

–You should be weeping all the time. And you *have* wept. You have suffered a great deal. And yet you are very happy. You wouldn't change places with anyone. For many years now you have not lost your *gaudium cum pace* – your peaceful joy. You thank God for this and would like to let everyone into the secret of your happiness.

–Yes, I can see why people have often said of you – though you couldn't care less about "what people say" – that you are "a man of peace".

175 Some people do only what lies within the capacity of poor human creatures to accomplish, and consequently waste their time. What Peter experienced is repeated once more, word for word: *Praeceptor, per totam noctem laborantes nihil cepimus.*

– Master, we have toiled all night and caught nothing.

If they work on their own, without being united with the Church, not reckoning with the Church, what possible effectiveness could their apostolate have? None at all!

–They need to be convinced that *on their own* they can achieve nothing. You should help them to go on listening to the rest of that Gospel story: *in verbo autem tuo laxabo rete* – at your word I will let down the net. It is then that the catch will be plentiful and effective.

–How beautiful it is to mend our ways when we find we have, for whatever reason, done apostolate on our own account!

176 It was you who wrote what I am now copying out: "*Domine, tu scis quia amo te!* – Lord, you know that I love you! How very often, Jesus, I repeat again and again those words your dear Cephas uttered, as a bitter-sweet litany. For I know that I love you, and yet I am so very unsure of myself that I cannot bring myself to say it to you clearly. There are so many denials in my wicked life. *Tu scis, Domine!* – You know that I love you! –May my actions, Jesus, never go against these yearnings of my heart."

–Keep up this prayer of yours and he will certainly hear you.

177 Repeat this with confidence: Lord, if only my tears had been contrite!

–Ask him humbly to grant you the sorrow you desire.

178 How villainous has been my behaviour and how unfaithful I have been to God's grace!

–My Mother, Refuge of sinners, pray for me. May I never again hinder God's work in my soul.

179 So close to Christ for so many years and… such a sinner!

–Does that intimacy of Jesus with you not make you sob?

180 It is not that I lack true joy; on the contrary… And yet, painfully aware of my unworthiness, it is only natural that I should cry out with Saint Paul, "wretched man that I am!"

–It is at such a time that you should increase your desire to tear down once and for all the barriers you yourself have set up.

181 Do not become alarmed or discouraged to discover that you have failings… and such failings!

–Struggle to uproot them. And as you do so, be convinced that it is even a good thing to be aware of all those weaknesses, for otherwise you would be proud. And pride separates us from God.

182 Be filled with wonder at God's goodness, because Christ wants to live in you… also when you are aware of all the weight of your poor wretchedness, of this poor flesh, of all the vileness of this poor clay.

–Yes, but then remember too that call from God: Jesus Christ, who is God and Man, understands me and looks after me, for he is my Brother and my Friend.

183 Your life is happy, very happy, though on occasions you feel a pang of sadness, and even experience almost constantly a real sense of weariness.

–Joy and affliction can go hand in hand like this, each in its own "man": the former in the new man, the latter in the old.

184 Humility is born of knowing God and knowing oneself.

185 Lord, I ask for a gift from you: Love… a Love that will cleanse me. – And another gift as well: self-knowledge so that I may be filled with humility.

186 The saints are those who struggle right to the end of their lives: those who always manage to get up each time they stumble, each time they fall, and courageously embark on their way once more with humility, love and hope.

187 If your mistakes make you more humble, if they make you reach out more urgently for God's helping hand, then they are a road to sanctity: *Felix culpa!* – O happy fault!, the Church sings.

188 Prayer – even my prayer! – is all-powerful.

189 Humility teaches each soul not to lose heart in the face of its own blunders.

–True humility leads us… to ask for forgiveness!

190 If I were a leper my mother would hug me. She would kiss my wounds without fear or hesitation.

–Well then, what would the Blessed Virgin Mary do? When we feel we are like lepers, all full of sores, we have to cry out: Mother! And the protection of our Mother will be like a kiss upon our wounds, which obtains our cure.

191 In the sacrament of Penance, Jesus forgives us.

–Christ's merits are applied to us there. It is for love of us that he is on the Cross with his arms stretched out, fastened to the wood more by the Love he has for us than by the nails.

192 If ever you fall, my son, go quickly

to Confession and seek spiritual guidance. Show your wound!, so that it gets properly healed and all possibility of infection is removed, even if doing this hurts you as much as having an operation.

193 Sincerity is indispensable if we are to achieve greater union with God.

–If you have an ugly "toad" inside you, my son, let it out! As I have always advised you, the first thing you must mention is what you wouldn't like anybody to know. Once the "toad" has been let out in Confession – how well one feels!

194 *Nam, et si ambulavero in medio umbrae mortis, non timebo mala* – though I should walk through the valley of the shadow of death, no evil will I fear. Neither my wretchedness nor the temptations of the enemy will worry me, *quoniam tu mecum es* – for you Lord are with me.

195 Just now, Jesus, when I was considering my wretchedness, I said to you: Allow yourself to be taken in by this son of yours, just like those good fathers, full of kindness, who put into the hands of their little children the presents they want to receive from them… knowing perfectly well that little children have nothing of their own.

–And what merriment of father and son, even though they are both in on the secret!

196 Jesus, my Love, to think that I could offend you again! *Tuus ego sum... salvum me fac.* – I am yours: save me!

197 You, who see yourself so badly lacking in virtues, in talents, in abilities... Do you not feel the desire to cry out like the blind Bartimaeus, "Jesus, Son of David, have pity on me!"?

–What a beautiful aspiration for you to say very often, "Lord, have pity on me!"

–He will hear you and come to your aid.

198 Foster a desire for atonement in your soul, so that you may acquire greater contrition each day.

199 If you are faithful you will be able to count yourself a conqueror.

–Even though you may lose some battles in your life, you will not know defeat. You can be sure that there is no such thing as failure, if you act with purity of intention and with a desire to fulfil the Will of God.

–And then, whether you win or lose, you will always triumph in the end, because you will have carried out your work with Love.

200 I am sure that God has listened to your humble and heartfelt plea: My Lord, I am not worried about "what people say". Forgive me for my unworthy life: May I be a saint!… But it's You alone I wish to please.

201 In a Christian's life *everything* has to be for God – even personal weaknesses, once they have been put right! The Lord understands and forgives them.

202 What have I done to you, Jesus, that you should love me so? I have offended you... and loved you.

–Loving you: this is what my life is going to be all about.

203 Surely all those consolations I receive from the Master are given me so that I may think of him all the time and serve him in little things, and so be able to serve him in great things.

–A resolution: to please my good Jesus in the tiniest details of my daily life.

204 We have to love God because our heart is made for love. That is why, if we don't give our heart to God, to Our Lady and Mother, to souls... with a pure affection, it will seek revenge… and will breed worms instead.

205 Tell Our Lord with your whole heart: In spite of all my wretchedness I am madly in Love!, I am drunk with Love!

206 From now on, truly sorrowful for my many falls, I shall remain, with God's help, always on the Cross.

207 What the flesh lost, the flesh

should pay back: be generous in your penance.

208 Invoke the Lord, and beg him for the spirit of penance of one who conquers himself every day, and offers him this constant victory unassumingly and perseveringly.

209 In your personal prayer, whenever you experience the weakness of the flesh you should repeat: Lord, give the Cross to this poor body of mine, which gets tired and rebellious!

210 How right that priest was when he preached, saying, "Jesus has forgiven me the great multitude of my sins in spite of my ingratitude. How generous he is! If the many sins of Mary Magdalen were forgiven because she loved greatly, many more have been forgiven me. What a great debt of love still remains for me to pay!"

Jesus, I'm ready to the point of madness and heroism! With the help of your grace, even if I have to die for you, Lord, I will never abandon you again.

211 Lazarus rose because he heard the voice of God and immediately wanted to get out of the situation he was in. If he hadn't *wanted* to move, he would just have died again.

A sincere resolution: to have faith in God always; to hope in God always; to love God always… he never abandons us, even if we are rotting away as Lazarus was.

212 Let us marvel at the lovable paradox of our Christian condition: it is our own wretchedness which leads us to seek refuge in God, to become "like unto God". With him we can do all things.

213 When you have fallen or when you find yourself overwhelmed by the weight of your wretchedness, repeat with a firm hope: Lord, see how ill I am; Lord, you who died on the Cross for love of me, come and heal me.

Be full of confidence, I insist. Keep on calling out to his most loving Heart. As he cured the lepers we read about in the Gospel, he will cure you.

214 Trust fully in God and have a greater desire each day never to run away from him.

215 Virgin Immaculate, my Mother!, do not abandon me. See how my poor heart is filled with tears. –I do not want to offend my God!

–I already know, and I trust I shall never forget, that I am worth nothing. My smallness and my loneliness weigh upon me so much! But... I am not alone. You, Sweet Lady, and my Father God will never leave me.

Faced with the rebellion of my flesh and the diabolical arguments against my Faith, I love Jesus and I believe: I do Love and do Believe.

Pessimism

216 With God's grace, you have to tackle and carry out the impossible… because anybody can do what is possible.

217 Reject your pessimism and don't allow those around you to be pessimistic. –God should be served with cheerfulness and abandonment.

218 Get rid of that human prudence which makes you so very cautious, so – sorry to be so blunt! – cowardly.

–Let us not be narrow-minded. Let us not be infantile men or women, who are nearsighted and lack a supernatural breadth of vision…! Could we be working for ourselves? Of course not!

Well then, let us say quite fearlessly: Dearest Jesus, we are working for you, and… are you going to deny us the material means we need? You know full well how worthless we are; still, I would not treat a servant working for me in that way…

Therefore, we hope and are sure you will give us all we need to be able to serve you.

219 An act of faith: Nothing can prevail against God! Nothing can prevail against God's people!

–Don't forget it.

220 Don't lose heart. Carry on! Carry on with that holy stubbornness which in spiritual terms is called *perseverance*.

221 My Lord, you always come to meet our real needs.

222 You are not getting worse. –It is just that now you have more light to see yourself as you really are. You must avoid even the slightest hint of discouragement.

223 Along the way to personal sanctity we can at times get the impression that we are going backwards instead of forwards, that we are getting worse instead of better.

As long as there is interior struggle this pessimistic thought is only an illusion, a deception to be rejected as false.

–Persevere and don't worry. If you fight with tenacity you are making progress and are growing in sanctity.

224 Interior dryness is not lukewarmness. When a person is lukewarm the waters of grace slide over him without being soaked in. In contrast, there are dry lands which seem arid but which, with a few drops of rain at the right time, yield abundant flowers and delicious fruit.

That is why I ask: When are we going to be convinced? How important it is to be docile to the divine calls which come at each moment of the day, because it is precisely there that God is awaiting us!

225 Be clever, spiritually clever. Don't wait for the Lord to send you setbacks; go out to meet them with a spirit of voluntary atonement. –Then you'll receive them not so much with resignation (an old-sounding word) as with Love – a word which is forever young.

226 Today, for the first time, you had the feeling that things were getting simpler, that everything was "sorting itself out". At last you see an end to the problems that were worrying you. And you understand that they are more thoroughly and better resolved the more you abandon yourself into the arms of your Father God.

What are you waiting for to start behaving always as a son of God? This should be the driving force in your life.

227 Turn to Our Lady – the Mother, Daughter and Spouse of God, and our Mother – and ask her to obtain more graces for you from the Blessed Trinity: the grace of faith, of hope, of love and of contrition. So that when it seems that a harsh dry wind is blowing in your life, threatening to wither those flowers of your soul, they will not wither… and neither will those of your brothers.

228 Be filled with faith and rest assured! The Lord tells us this through the prophet Jeremiah: *orabitis me, et ego exaudiam vos* – whenever you call upon me, whenever you pray!, I will listen to you.

229 I refer everything to you, my God. Without you – who are my Father – what would become of me?

230 Allow me to give you the advice of an experienced soul: your prayer – and your whole life should be to pray always – ought to be as trusting as "a child's prayer".

231 A sick man is brought to Jesus, who looks at him. – Contemplate the scene closely and meditate on his words: *confide, fili* – take heart, my son.

This is what Our Lord says to you when you feel the weight of your errors. Have faith! In the first place: faith. And then allow yourself to be carried like the paralytic did: with interior and submissive obedience!

232 My son, you can do nothing on the supernatural level through your own strength; whereas when you become God's instrument you can do everything. *Omnia possum in eo qui me confortat!* – I can do all things in him who strengthens me. For in his goodness he wishes to use inadequate instruments, like you and like me.

233 Whenever you pray, make the effort to have the kind of faith of those sick people we read about in the Gospel. You can be sure Jesus is listening to you.

234 My Mother! Mothers on earth look with greater love on the weakest of their children, the one with the worst health, or who is least intelligent, or is a poor cripple…

–Sweet Lady! I know that you are more of a Mother than all other mothers put together. –And, since I am your son… And, since I am weak, and ill… and crippled… and ugly...

235 We lack faith. The day we practise this virtue, trusting in God and in his Mother, we will be courageous and loyal.

God, who is the same God as ever, will work miracles through our hands.

–Grant me, dear Jesus, the faith I truly desire! My Mother, sweet Lady, Mary most holy, make me believe!

236 A firm resolution: to abandon myself in Jesus Christ with all my wretchedness. Whatever he may want, at any moment, *Fiat* – let it be done!

237 Never lose heart, for Our Lord is always ready to give you the necessary grace for the new conversion you need, for that ascent in the supernatural field.

238 "Blessed be God!" you said to yourself after having finished your sacramental Confession. And you thought: it is as if I had just been born again.

You then continued calmly: "*Domine, quid me vis facere?* – Lord, what would you have me do?"

–And you yourself came up with the reply: "With the help of your grace I will let nothing and no one come between me and the fulfilment of your most Holy Will:

Serviam – I will serve you unconditionally!"

239 We read in the Gospel that the Magi, *videntes stellam* – when they saw the star – were filled with great joy.

–They rejoiced, my son, they were immensely glad, because they had done what they were supposed to do; and they rejoiced because they knew for certain they would reach the King, who never abandons those who seek him.

240 When you really come to love God's Will you will never, even in the worst state of agitation, lose sight of the fact that our Father in Heaven is always close to you, very close, right next to you, with his everlasting Love and with his unbounded affection.

241 If the outlook in your interior life, in your soul, is darkened, allow yourself to be led along by the hand, as a blind man would do.

–In time the Lord will reward this humble surrendering of your own judgement by giving you clarity of mind.

242 To be afraid of anything or anybody, but especially of the person who directs our soul, is unworthy of a son of God.

243 Are you not moved to hear some affectionate word addressed to your mother?

–Well, the same thing happens to Our Lord. We cannot separate Jesus from his Mother.

244 When you find yourself tired and exhausted, approach Our Lord confidently, as that good friend of ours did, and say: "Jesus, see what you can do about it. Even before I begin to fight, I am already tired."

–He will give you his strength.

245 A task which presents no difficulties lacks human appeal – and supernatural appeal too. If you find no resistance when hammering a nail into a wall, what can you expect to hang on it?

246 It seems incredible that a man like you – who say you know you're nothing – should dare to place obstacles in the way of God's grace.

Yet this is what you're doing with your false humility, your "objectivity", your pessimism.

247 Lord, grant me the grace to give up everything that has to do with myself. I should have no other concern than your Glory… in other words, your Love. –Everything for Love!

248 "When Herod heard this," (that the King had come to this earth), "he was troubled, and all Jerusalem with him."

This is an every day occurrence! We see the same thing happening now. In the face of God's greatness, which shows itself in a thousand ways, there are always some people – sometimes even in positions of authority – who are troubled. It's because they do not love God; because they have no real wish to meet him; because they don't want to follow his inspirations, and so they become obstacles in God's path.

–Be forewarned; carry on working, don't worry, seek the Lord, pray… and he will triumph.

249 You are not alone. –Neither you nor I can ever find ourselves alone. And even less if we go to Jesus through Mary, for she is a Mother who will never abandon us.

250 When it feels as if the Lord has given up on you, don't give way to sadness Seek him with greater determination! He who is Love does not leave you on your own.

–Be convinced that "he has left you on your own" out of Love, so that you may see clearly in your life what is his and what is yours.

251 You said to me: "I seem not only unable to go ahead along my way, but also unable to be saved without a miracle of grace. Oh, my poor soul! I remain cold and, what is worse, almost indifferent. It's as if I were an outsider looking at 'a case' (mine) which had nothing to do with him. Will these days turn out to be completely futile?

And nevertheless, my Mother is my Mother and Jesus is – dare I say it? – *my* Jesus. And there are good and saintly souls, at this very moment, praying for me."

–Go on walking hand in hand with

your Mother, I replied, and "dare" to say to Jesus that he is yours. In his goodness he will bring clear light to your soul.

252 Grant me, Jesus, the Cross with no Simon of Cyrene to help me. No, that's not right; I need your grace, I need your help here as in everything. You must be my Simon of Cyrene. With you, my God, no trial can daunt me…

–But what if my Cross should consist in boredom or sadness? – In that case I say to you, Lord, with You I would gladly be sad.

253 As long as I don't lose You, no sorrow will be a sorrow at all.

254 Jesus will refuse a word to no one, and his words bring healing, they console, they bring light.

–This is what you and I have to remember at all times, especially when we find ourselves tired and weighed down by work or opposition.

255 Don't expect people's applause for your work.

–What is more, sometimes you mustn't even expect other people and institutions, who like you are working for Christ, to understand you.

–Seek only the glory of God and, while loving everyone, don't worry if there are some who don't understand you.

256 If there are mountains in the way, obstacles, misunderstandings and back-biting, which Satan seeks and God allows, you must have faith, faith with deeds, faith with sacrifice, faith with humility.

257 Faced by apparent sterility in your apostolate you begin to detect the first waves of discouragement, which your faith rejects quite firmly. –But you realise that you need a more humble, lively and operative faith.

As someone who longs to bring health to souls, you should cry out like the father of that sick boy possessed by the devil: *Domine, adiuva incredulitatem meam!* – Lord, help my unbelief!

Have no doubt: the miracle will be performed again.

258 What a beautiful prayer for you to say frequently, that one of our good friend praying for a priest whom hatred for religion imprisoned: "My God, comfort him, since it is for you he suffers persecution. How many suffer, because they serve you!"

–What a source of joy the Communion of Saints is!

259 The measures taken by some governments to ensure that the faith in their countries dies out reminds me of the seals set upon the tomb of Jesus by the Sanhedrin.

–He was not subject to anybody or anything, and despite those seals, he rose again!

260 The solution is to love. Saint John the Apostle wrote some words which really move me: *qui autem timet, non est perfectus in caritate*. I like to translate them as follows, almost word for word – the fearful man doesn't know how to love.

–You, therefore, who do love and know how to show it, you mustn't be afraid of anything. So, on you go!

261 God is with you. The Blessed Trinity dwells in your soul in grace.

–That is why, in spite of your wretchedness, you can and should keep up a continuous conversation with the Lord.

262 You should pray at all times, always. –You should feel the need to go to God after every success and after every failure in your interior life.

263 May your prayer always be a real and sincere act of adoration of God.

264 When the Lord brought you into the Church he put an indelible mark upon your soul through Baptism: you are a son of God. – Don't forget it.

265 Give thanks often to Jesus, for through him, with him and in him you are able to call yourself a son of God.

266 If we feel we are beloved sons of our Heavenly Father, as indeed we are!, how can we fail to be happy all the time? –Think about it.

267 As he was giving out Holy Communion that priest felt like shouting out: this is Happiness I am giving to you!

268 Build up a gigantic faith in the Holy Eucharist. –Be filled with wonder before this ineffable reality! We have God with us; we can receive him every day and, if we want to, we can speak intimately with him, just as we talk with a friend, as we talk with a brother, as we talk with a father, as we talk with Love itself.

269 How beautiful our Christian vocation is – to be sons of God! It brings joy and peace on earth which the world cannot give!

270 Lord, grant me the love with which you want me to love you.

271 That morning, to remove the dark shadow of pessimism which hung over you, you also insisted as you do every day… but you were more "aggressive" with your Angel. You sang his praises and you asked him to teach you to love Jesus at least, at least as much as *he* loves Him… And with that you recovered your calm.

272 Ask your Mother Mary, ask Saint Joseph and your Guardian Angel to speak to the Lord and tell him the things you can't manage to put into words because you are so dull.

273 Fill yourself with confidence. The Mother we have is the Mother of God, the Most Blessed Virgin, the Queen of Heaven and the World.

274 Jesus was born in a cave in Bethlehem because, Sacred Scripture tells us, "there was no room for them in the inn."

–I am not departing from theological truth when I say that Jesus is still looking for shelter in your heart.

275 Our Lord is on the Cross saying, I am suffering so that men, who are my brothers, may be happy, not only in Heaven, but also – as far as possible – on earth, if they really embrace the most Holy Will of my heavenly Father.

276 It is true that your contribution is nil and that it is God who does everything in your soul.

–However, let not this be the case as far as your correspondence to his grace is concerned.

277 Practise the virtue of hope and, with God as your motive, even when you find it hard, persevere at your work and try to finish it well, convinced that those efforts of yours are not useless in the Lord's sight.

278 When in your daily struggle, normally made up of many little things, there is the desire and the reality of pleasing God continually, I assure you: nothing is ever lost!

279 You would be right in thinking: how good the Lord is, who has sought me and has made known to me this holy path where I can be effective and where I can love all men, bringing them peace and happiness.

–This thought has then to be turned into resolutions.

280 You know that you will never lack God's grace, because he has chosen you from all eternity. And if this is what he has done for you, he will grant you all the help you need to be faithful to him as his son.

–Go forward, then, with assurance and try to respond at every moment.

281 I ask the Mother of God to smile upon us if she wishes, if she can... She will indeed do so.

Moreover, she will reward our generosity a thousandfold here on earth. A thousandfold, that's what I am asking her for!

282 Practise a cheerful charity which is at once kindly and firm; human and supernatural. An affectionate charity, knowing how to welcome everyone with a sincere and habitual smile, and how to understand the ideas and the feelings of others.

–In this way, gently and vigorously, and without concessions in matters of personal morals or in doctrine, the charity of Christ – when it is being well lived – will give you a spirit of conquest. Each day you will be more eager to work for souls.

283 My son, I said with assurance, in spreading our "madness" to other apostles I am not unaware of the "obstacles" we will find. Some of them may appear insurmountable... But *inter medium montium pertransibunt aquae* – the waters will pass through the midst of the mountains. Our supernatural spirit and the drive of our zeal will cut through the mountains and we shall overcome those obstacles.

284 "My God, my God! All of them were equally loved, through you, in you and with you, and now they are all scattered." Thus you complained when you saw yourself once again all alone and lacking in human resources.

–But Our Lord immediately made you feel sure in your soul that He would sort it out. And you said to him: "You will fix everything."

–And so he did. God solved everything sooner, more fully and better than you expected.

285 It is indeed just that the Father, the Son and the Holy Spirit should crown the Blessed Virgin as Queen and Lady of all created things.

–You have to make use of her power! With the daring of a child join in this celebration in Heaven. – For myself, I crown the Mother of God and my Mother with my purified failings, since I have no precious stones or virtues.

–Take courage!

You can!

286 I want to warn you against a difficulty that may arise: it is the temptation of weariness and discouragement.

–Isn't it still fresh in your memory what life – your old life – used to be like, with no aim to it, no purpose, no sparkle, and then, with God's light and your own dedication, a new direction was given to it and you were filled with joy?

–Don't be so silly as to exchange your new life for that other one.

287 If you feel for whatever reason that you cannot manage, abandon yourself in God, telling him: Lord, I trust in you, I abandon myself in you, but do help me in my weakness!

And filled with confidence, repeat: See Jesus what a filthy rag I am. My life seems to me so miserable. I am not worthy to be a son of yours. Tell him all this – and tell him so over and over again.

–It will not be long before you hear him say, *Ne timeas!* – do not be afraid; and also: *Surge et ambula!* – rise up and walk!

288 You were still rather hesitant when you were telling me: "I am deeply aware of the occasions when the Lord is asking more of me."

–All I could think of was to remind you how you used to assure me that the only thing you wanted was to identify yourself with him. What's keeping you back?

289 If only you could manage to fulfil that resolution you made: "to die a little to myself each day."

290 Joy, and supernatural and human optimism, can go hand in hand with physical tiredness, with sorrow, with tears (because we have a heart), and with difficulties in our interior life or our apostolic work.

He who is *perfectus Deus, perfectus Homo* – perfect God and perfect Man – and who enjoyed every happiness in Heaven, chose to experience fatigue and tiredness, tears and suffering... so that we might understand that if we are to be supernatural we must also be very human.

291 Jesus is asking you to pray … You see this very clearly.

–Nonetheless, how poor your response has been! Everything is a great effort for you: you are like a baby who is too lazy to learn to walk. But in your case it isn't just laziness. It is fear, too, and a lack of generosity!

292 You should repeat very often: Jesus, if ever a doubt creeps into my soul, setting up other noble ambitions in place of what you are asking of me, I tell you now that I prefer to follow you, no matter how much it costs. Do not leave me!

293 Seek union with God and buoy yourself up with hope – that *sure* virtue! –

because Jesus will illuminate the way for you with the light of his mercy, even in the darkest night.

294 Your prayer went like this: "My wretchedness weighs me down, but it doesn't overwhelm me because I am a son of God. I want to atone, to Love... And," you added, "like Saint Paul, I want to turn my weaknesses to good use, convinced that the Lord will not abandon those who place their trust in him."

–Carry on like that. I assure you that – with God's grace – you will succeed, and you will overcome your wretchedness and your shortcomings.

295 Any time is the right time to make an effective resolution, to say "I believe", to say "I hope", to say "I love".

296 Learn to praise the Father, the Son and the Holy Spirit. Learn to have a special devotion to the Blessed Trinity: I believe in God the Father, I believe in God the Son, I believe in God the Holy Spirit; I hope in God the Father, I hope in God the Son, I hope in God the Holy Spirit; I love God the Father, I love God the Son, I love God the Holy Spirit. I believe, I hope and I love the most Holy Trinity.

–This devotion is much needed as a supernatural exercise for the soul, expressed by the movement of the heart, although not always in words.

297 The system, the method, the procedure, the only way to have a life abundant and fertile in supernatural fruits, is to follow the Holy Spirit's advice, which comes to us via the *Acts of the Apostles*: *omnes erant perseverantes unanimiter in oratione* – all these with one accord devoted themselves to prayer.

–*Nothing* can be done without prayer!

298 My Lord Jesus has a Heart more tender than the hearts of all good men put together. If a good man (of average goodness) knew that a certain person loved him, without seeking personal satisfaction or reward of any kind (he loves for love's sake); and if he also knew that all this person wanted from him was that he should not object to being loved, even from afar... then it would not be long before he responded to such a disinterested love.

–If the Loved One is so powerful that he can do all things, I am sure that, as well as surrendering in the end to the faithful love of a creature (in spite of the wretchedness of that poor soul) he will give this lover the supernatural beauty, knowledge and power he needs so that the eyes of Jesus are not sullied when he gazes upon the poor heart that is adoring him.

–Love, my child; love and hope.

299 If there is sacrifice when you sow Love, you will also reap Love.

300 My child, are you not aflame with the desire to bring all men to love Him?

301 Jesus as a child, Jesus as an adolescent. I love to picture you like this, Lord, because… I can dare more. I love to see you as a tiny, almost helpless babe. It makes me feel you need me.

302 Whenever I go into the oratory,

having become a little child once more, I say to Our Lord that I love him more than anyone.

303 How wonderfully effective the Holy Eucharist is in the action – and even before that, in the spirit – of those who receive it frequently and piously.

304 If all those people became so enthusiastic and were ready to acclaim you over a piece of bread, even though the multiplication was a very great miracle, shouldn't we be doing much more for all the many gifts you have granted us, and especially for giving us your very self unreservedly in the Eucharist?

305 Good child: see how lovers on earth kiss the flowers, the letters, the mementos of those they love...

–Then you, how could you ever forget that you have him always at your side... yes, *Him!*? – How could you forget... that you can eat him?

306 Put your head frequently round the

oratory door to say to Jesus… I abandon myself into your arms.

–Leave everything you have – your wretchedness! – at his feet.

–In this way, in spite of the welter of things you carry along behind you, you will never lose your peace.

307 Pray resolutely using the words of the Psalmist: "Lord, you are my refuge and my strength, I trust in thee!"

I promise you that he will preserve you from the ambushes of the "noontide devil", when you are tempted and… even when you fall, and when your age and virtues ought to have proved solid and you should have known by heart that He alone is your Strength.

308 Do you think people are grateful for services rendered only reluctantly? Evidently not. You might even say it would have been better not to have bothered.

–And yet you think you can serve God with sour looks? No! –You have to serve him cheerfully, in spite of your wretchedness, which we will be able to get rid of with

God's grace.

309 Doubts assail you, temptations, with that gloss of elegance about them.

–I love to hear you say how this shows that the devil considers you his enemy, and that God's grace will never leave you unprotected. Keep up the struggle!

310 The majority of people who have personal problems "have them" because they selfishly think about themselves.

311 Everything seems so peaceful. God's enemy, however, is not asleep...

–The Heart of Jesus is also awake and watching! There lies my hope.

312 Sanctity is to be found in struggling, in knowing that we have defects and in heroically trying to overcome them.

Sanctity, I insist, consists in overcoming those defects... although we will still have defects when we die; because if not, as I have told you, we would become proud.

313 Thank you, Lord, because – as well

as allowing us to be tempted – you also give us the strength and beauty of your grace so that we can win through! Thank you, Lord, for the temptations you allow us to have so that we may be humble!

314 Do not abandon me, Lord. Don't you see the bottomless pit this poor son of yours would end up in?

–My Mother: I am your son too.

315 It is impossible to live a clean life without God's help. God wants us to be humble, and to ask him for his help through our Mother who is his Mother.

You should say to Our Lady, right now, speaking without the sound of words, from the accompanied solitude of your heart: "O, my Mother, sometimes this poor heart of mine rebels… But if you help me..." – She will indeed help you to keep it clean and to follow the way God has called you to pursue. The Virgin Mary will always make it easier for you to fulfil the Will of God.

316 To preserve holy purity and live a

clean life you have to love and practise daily mortification.

317 Whenever you feel the stirrings of your poor flesh, which sometimes attacks with violent assaults, kiss your crucifix, *kiss it many times* with firm resolve, even if it seems to you that you are doing so without love.

318 Place yourself before the Lord each day and tell him slowly and in all earnestness, like the man in the Gospel who was in such great need, *Domine, ut videam!* – Lord, that I may see!; that I may see what you expect from me, and struggle to be faithful to you.

319 My God, how easy it is to persevere when we know that You are the Good Shepherd, and that we – you and I… – are sheep belonging to your flock!

–For we know full well that the Good Shepherd gives his whole life for each one of his sheep.

320 Today in your prayer you

confirmed your resolution to be a saint. I understand you when you make this more specific by adding, "I know I shall succeed, not because I am sure of myself, Jesus, but because… I am sure of you."

321 By yourself, if you don't count on grace, you can do nothing worthwhile, for you would be cutting the link which connects you with God.

–With grace, on the other hand, you can do all things.

322 Do you want to learn from Christ and follow the example of his life? –Open the Holy Gospels and listen to God in dialogue with men… with you.

323 Jesus knows very well what is best... and I love his Will and will do so always. He it is who controls "the puppets" and so, provided it is a means to achieving our end, even if there are godless men who are determined to put obstacles in the way, he will grant what I am asking.

324 True faith shows itself in humility.

Dicebat enim intra se – that poor woman said to herself: *Si tetigero tantum vestimentum eius, salva ero* – if I can but touch the hem of his garment, I shall be healed.

–What humility she showed, a result and a sign of her faith!

325 If God gives you the burden, God will give you the strength.

326 Invoke the Holy Spirit in your examination of conscience so that you may get to know God better, and yourself also. In this way you will be converted each day.

327 Spiritual direction. Don't object to someone poking at your soul with supernatural sense and holy shamelessness to check how true it is that you are able – *and willing* – to give glory to God.

328 *Quomodo fiet istud quoniam virum non cognosco?* – How can this marvel take place if I have no knowledge of man? What Mary asks the Angel is a reflection of her sincere Heart.

Observing the Blessed Virgin has confirmed for me a clear rule of conduct: to enjoy peace, and to live in peace, we must be very sincere with God, with those who direct our souls and with ourselves.

329 A foolish child wails and stamps his feet when his loving mother puts a needle to his finger to get a splinter out... A sensible child, perhaps with his eyes full of tears – for the flesh is weak – looks gratefully at his good mother who is making him suffer a little in order to avoid much greater harm.

–Jesus, may I be a sensible child.

330 My child, my little donkey: if the Lord, with Love, has washed your grimy back, so accustomed to the muck, and has laid a satin harness on you, and covered you with dazzling jewels, don't forget, poor donkey, that with your faults you *could* throw that beautiful load on to the ground... But on your own you *couldn't* put it back on again.

331 Rest in divine filiation. God is a Father – your Father! – full of warmth and infinite love.

–Call him Father frequently and tell him, when you are alone, that you love him, that you love him very much!, and that you feel proud and strong because you are his son.

332 Cheerfulness is a necessary consequence of our divine filiation, of knowing that our Father God loves us with a love of predilection, that he welcomes us, helps us and forgives us.

–Remember this and never forget it: even if it should seem at times that everything is collapsing, *nothing* is collapsing at all, because God doesn't lose battles.

333 The best way of showing our gratitude to God is to be passionately in love with the fact that we are his children.

334 You are like the little pauper who suddenly finds out that he is the son of the King. That is why now the only thing that concerns you on this earth is the Glory of your Father God, his Glory in everything.

335 My little friend, say to him: Jesus, knowing that I love you and that you love me, nothing else matters: all is well.

336 "I have asked Our Lady for many things," you were telling me, and then you corrected yourself: "What I should say is that I have brought many things to Our Lady's attention."

337 "I can do all things in him who strengthens me." With him there is no possibility of failure, and this conviction gives rise to the holy "superiority complex" whereby we take on things with a spirit of victory, because God grants us his strength.

338 The artist stood before his canvas with a deep desire to surpass himself and cried out, "Lord, I want to paint for you thirty-eight hearts, thirty-eight angels bursting with continual love for you, thirty-eight marvels embroidered on your heaven, thirty-eight suns upon your mantle, thirty-eight flames of fire, thirty-eight ardours, thirty-eight feats of madness, thirty-eight joys..."

Then, humbly, he had to admit that it was all in his imagination and desire. In reality what confronts him are thirty-eight figures which haven't come out properly and which mortify the sight rather than give pleasure.

339 We have no right to claim that the Angels should obey us... but we can be absolutely sure that the Holy Angels hear us always.

340 Allow God to lead you. He will lead you along "his path", making use of innumerable adversities... possibly including your own sluggishness, so that it may clearly be seen that your work is being carried out by him.

341 Ask him without any fear, and insist. Remember that scene of the multiplication of loaves we read about in the Gospel. Notice how magnanimously he says to the Apostles, How many loaves do you have? Five?... How many are you asking for?... And he gives six, a hundred, thousands... Why?

–Because Christ sees all our needs with divine wisdom, and with his almighty power he can and does go far beyond our desires.

Our Lord sees much farther than our poor minds can discern and he is infinitely generous!

342 When we're working for God we have to have a "superiority complex", I told you.

But isn't that a sign of pride? you asked me. –No! It is a consequence of humility; the humility which makes me say: Lord, you are who you are. I am nothingness itself. You have all the perfections: power, strength, love, glory, wisdom, authority, dignity... If I unite myself to you, like a child who goes to the strong arms of his father or the wonderful lap of his mother, I will feel the warmth of your divinity, I will feel the light of your wisdom, I will feel your strength coursing through my veins.

343 If you are aware of God's presence, high above the deafening storm, the sun will always be shining on you; and deep below the roaring and destructive waves, peace and calm will reign in your soul.

344 For a son of God each day should be an opportunity for renewal, knowing for sure that with the help of grace he will reach the end of the road, which is Love.

That is why if you begin and begin again, you are doing well. If you have a will to win, if you struggle, then, with God's help, you will conquer! There will be no difficulty you cannot overcome!

345 Make your way to Bethlehem, go up to the Child, take him in your arms and dance, say warm and tender things to him, press him close to your heart...

–I am not talking childish nonsense: I am speaking of love! And love is shown with deeds. In the intimacy of your soul, you can indeed hug him tight!

346 We should let Jesus know that we are children. And when children are tiny and innocent, what a lot of effort it takes for them to go up one step. They look as though they are wasting their time, but eventually they manage to climb up. Now there is another step. Crawling on their hands and knees, and putting their whole body into it, they score another success... one more step. Then they start again. What an effort! There are only a few more steps to go now... But then the toddler stumbles... and – whoops! – down he goes. With bumps all over and in floods of tears, the poor child sets out and begins to try again.

We are just like that, Jesus, when we are on our own. Please take us up in your loving arms, like a big and good Friend of the simple child. Do not leave us until we have reached the top. And then – oh then! – we will know how to correspond to your Merciful Love, with the daring of young children, telling you, sweet Lord, that after Mary and Joseph, there never has been nor will there ever be a mortal soul – and there have been some who have been really crazy – who loves you as much as I love you.

347 Don't be ashamed of doing little childlike things, I advised you. As long as they are not done out of routine, they will not be fruitless.

–For example: Imagine that a soul who is following the way of spiritual childhood is moved each night, during the hours of sleep, to wrap up a wooden statue of the Blessed Virgin.

Our intelligence would reject such an action as quite useless. But a soul, touched by grace, understands very well that a child would indeed act like this out of love.

And then the strong will, which all those who are spiritually tiny have, insists and moves the intelligence to give way... And if that childlike soul were to continue each day wrapping up the statue of Our Lady, there would be repeated each day a little childlike act which would be fruitful in the eyes of God.

348 When you are genuinely a child and you follow the ways of childhood – if you are moved by God to follow this path – you will be invincible.

349 The confident petition of a small child: Grant me, Lord, the sort of compunction which those who have pleased you most have had.

350 Small child, you would cease to be one if anyone or anything came between you and God.

351 I shouldn't ask Jesus for anything. I will concentrate on pleasing him in everything and telling him things as though he didn't know them already, just as a little child does with his father.

352 Little child, say to Jesus: I will not be satisfied with anything less than You.

353 In your prayer of spiritual childhood what childish things you say to your Lord! With the confidence of a child speaking to his great Friend of whose love he is utterly sure, you confided in him, saying, May I live only for your Glory!

Thinking things over you admit in all sincerity that everything you do turns out badly. "But," you add, "this can't surprise you, Jesus. It is impossible for me to do anything right. You have to help me. Please do it for me and you will see how well it turns out."

Then, with great daring, and without

departing from the truth, you continue: "May your Spirit thoroughly penetrate me and intoxicate me so that I may be able to do your Will. I want to do it. And if I don't do it... it's because you are not helping me. But you *are* helping me!"

354 You have to feel the urgent necessity to see yourself as small, weak and bereft of everything. You will then throw yourself onto the lap of our Mother in Heaven, with heartfelt aspirations and loving glances, Marian devotions... which are such a vital part of your filial spirit.

–She will watch over you.

355 Persevere along your way no matter what happens; persevere, cheerfully and optimistically, because the Lord is bent on sweeping aside all obstacles.

–Hear me well: I am quite certain that if you struggle, you will be a saint!

356 The first Apostles, when Our Lord called them, were by the side of an old boat busy mending the torn nets. Our Lord told them to follow him and *statim* – immediately

– *relictis omnibus* – they left everything – everything! And followed him...

And it does happen sometimes that we, who wish to imitate them, don't quite leave everything, and there remains some attachment in our heart, something wrong in our life which we're not willing to break with and offer it up to God.

–Won't you examine your heart in depth? Nothing should remain there except what is his. If not, we aren't really loving him, neither you nor I.

357 Tell Our Lord constantly and sincerely that you desire to be a saint and to do apostolate... Then the poor vessel of your soul will not get broken. And should it do so, it will be put together again and acquire an added attractiveness, and it will continue to be of use for your sanctity and the apostolate.

358 Your prayer should be that of a child of God, and not that of the hypocrites who will hear from Jesus' lips: "Not every one who says to me, Lord, Lord, shall enter into the Kingdom of Heaven."

Your prayer, your clamour of "Lord, Lord" should be linked in a thousand different ways throughout the day to a desire and an effective effort to fulfil the Will of God.

359 Little one, say to him: O Jesus, I don't want the devil to get hold of souls!

360 If God's Love has chosen you out and called you to follow him, you have a duty to respond to him... and it is also your duty, an equally serious duty, to lead and to contribute to the holiness and good progress of other men, your brothers.

361 Cheer up!... Not least when the going gets hard. Doesn't it make you happy to think that your faithfulness to your Christian commitments depends to a large extent on you?

Be full of joy and freely renew your decision: "Lord, I want it too. Count on the little I have to offer."

362 God is not removing you from your environment. He is not taking you away from the world, or from your condition in life, or from your noble human ambitions, or from your professional work... But he wants you to be a saint – right there!

363 Putting yourself in the presence of God, and with your forehead flat against the ground, consider how (for that's the way it is) you are more filthy and despicable than the sweepings swept up by a broom.

–And, in spite of this, the Lord has chosen you.

364 –When are you going to make up your mind!

Many people around you live a life of sacrifice simply for human reasons. These poor people forget they are children of God and act the way they do perhaps only out of pride, or to excel, or to be more comfortably off later on in life. They give up all kinds of things!

And you, who carry the sweet burden of the Church, of your family, your colleagues and friends, motives for which it is worthwhile sacrificing yourself, what are you doing about it? With what sense of responsibility are you reacting?

365 "O Lord, why did you come looking for me – who am useless – when there are so many people who are holy, wise, rich and full of prestige?"

–You are right... and precisely because of that you should be grateful to him with deeds and love.

366 Jesus, may everyone in your Holy Church persevere in their way, following their Christian vocation, like the Wise Men who followed the star, spurning Herod's advice – that will not be lacking.

367 Let us ask Jesus Christ that the fruits of his Redemption may grow abundantly in souls: more and more, ever more abundantly – divinely abundantly!

And for this to be so, may he make us good children of his Blessed Mother.

368 Would you like to know a secret to happiness? Give yourself to others and serve them, without waiting to be thanked.

369 Live and work for God, with a spirit of love and service, with a priestly soul, even though you may not be a priest. Then all your actions will take on a genuine supernatural meaning which will keep your whole life united to the source of all graces.

370 Looking on the immense panorama of souls who are awaiting us, and being struck by the wonderful and awesome responsibility before us, you may at times have asked yourself, as I have: "Can I contribute anything, when the task is so vast? I, who am so puny?"

–It is then we have to open the Gospel and contemplate how Jesus cures the man born blind. He uses mud made from the dust of the earth and saliva. Yet this is the salve which brings light to those blind eyes!

That is what you and I are. Fully aware of our weaknesses and our worthlessness, but with the grace of God and our good will, we can be salve to give light and provide strength for others as well as for ourselves.

371 Said an apostolic soul: Jesus, You know what needs to be done... you know I am not working for myself...

372 If you persevere in your prayer, with "personal perseverance", God Our Lord will give you all the means you need to be more effective and to spread his kingdom in the world.

–But you have to keep faithful: asking, asking, asking... Are you really behaving this way?

373 The Lord wants his children in all the honest pathways of this earth, sowing the seeds of understanding and forgiveness, of harmony, charity and peace.

–How about you? What are you doing?

374 The Redemption is still being accomplished, even now... and you are – you *have* to be – a co-redeemer.

375 To be a Christian in the world doesn't mean isolating oneself – on the contrary! It means loving all mankind and burning with a desire to enkindle in everyone the fire of the love of God.

376 Dear Lady, Mother of God and my Mother, not in the remotest way do I wish that you may ever be anything less than Mistress and Empress of the whole of creation.

TO FIGHT ONCE MORE

377 Follow Saint Paul's advice: *hora est iam nos de somno surgere!* – it is time to get down to work! Both on the inside, building up your soul; and on the outside, right where you are, building up the Kingdom of God.

378 All contrite you told me: "How much wretchedness I see in myself! I am so stupid and I am carting around such a weight of concupiscence that it is as though I had never really done anything to get closer to God. O Lord, here I am beginning, beginning, always just beginning! I will try, however, to push forward each day with all my heart."

–May he bless those efforts of yours.

379 Father, you told me, I have committed many errors, I have made so many mistakes.

–I know, I replied. But God Our Lord, who also knows all that and has taken it into account, only asks you to be humble enough to admit it and asks that you struggle to make amends, so as to serve him better each day with more interior life, with continual prayer and with piety, and making use of the proper means to sanctify your work.

380 Would that you could acquire, as I know you would like to, the virtues of the donkey! Donkeys are humble, hard-working, persevering – stubborn! – and faithful, with a sure step, tough and – if they have a good master – also grateful and obedient.

381 Continue thinking about the donkey's good qualities and notice how in order to do anything worth while, it has to allow itself to be ruled by the will of whoever is leading it... On its own the donkey would only... make an ass of itself. Probably the brightest thing that would occur to it to do would be to roll over on the ground, trot to the manger and start braying.

"Dear Jesus", you too should say to him, "*ut iumentum factus sum apud te!* – you have made me be your little donkey. Please don't leave me: *et ego semper tecum!* – and I will stay with you always. Lead me, tightly harnessed by your grace: *Tenuisti manum dexteram meam...* – you have led me by the halter; *et in voluntate tua deduxisti me...* – make me do your Will. And so I will love you for ever and ever – *et cum gloria suscepisti me!*"

382 Even the most insignificant mortification seems an epic to you. Sometimes Jesus uses your "peculiarities" and silly little fads, to help you mortify yourself, by making virtue out of necessity.

383 Dear Jesus, I do want to correspond to your Love, but I am so feeble.

–With your grace, I will know how to!

384 Spiritual life is – and I repeat this again and again, on purpose – a constant beginning and beginning again.

–Beginning again? Yes! Every time you make an act of contrition – and we should make many every day – you begin again, because you offer a new love to God.

385 We can never be content with what we are doing to serve our God, just as an artist is never satisfied with the painting or statue he is working on. Everyone tells him how marvellous it is, but he thinks: "No. It isn't quite right. I wanted it to be better." This is how we should feel.

Moreover, the Lord has given us so much. He has a right to the very best from us... and we must go at his pace.

386 You lack faith... and you lack love. Were it not so you would go immediately and much more often to Jesus, asking for this thing and that.

–Don't delay any further; call out to him and you will hear Christ speaking to you: "What do you want me to do for you?" Just as when he stopped for that poor blind man by the roadside who continued to insist, without giving up.

387 That good friend of ours wrote: "Many times I have asked the Lord to forgive me my very great sins. Kissing the Crucifix, I have told him that I love him and I have thanked him for his fatherly providence during these days. I was rather surprised, as I had been years ago, when I found myself saying (I didn't realise it until later): *Dei perfecta sunt opera* – all the works of God are perfect. At the same time I was left with the complete certainty, without the slightest doubt, that this reply to his sinful yet loving creature came from my God. All my hope is in him! May he be blessed for ever!!"

I hastened to reply: "The Lord always acts as the good Father he is, and gives us continual proofs of his Love. Place all your hope in him... and keep up your struggle."

388 O Jesus! If in spite of the poor way I have behaved, you have done for me what you have done..., what would you do if I were to respond well?

This truth will lead you to be generous without respite.

Weep, and grieve with sorrow and love, for Our Lord and his Blessed Mother deserve different treatment from you.

389 Even though at times you feel a deep distaste and you think you are only saying things with your lips, nevertheless keep up your acts of faith and hope and love. Don't fall asleep. Otherwise, when things are going fine, an ill wind will come and it will drag you off.

390 This is how you should pray: If I am to do anything worthwhile, Jesus, you will have to do it for me. May your Will be done. I do love it, even if your Will should permit that I be always as I am now, falling dismally only to be lifted up by you!

391 Make me into a saint, my God, even if you have to beat me into it. I don't want to be a hindrance to your Will. I want to respond, I want to be generous... But what sort of a wanting is mine?

392 You are full of concern because you do not love as you ought. Everything annoys you. And the enemy does all he can to make you show your bad temper.

–I realise you feel very humiliated. Precisely because of this you must take measures to react without delay.

393 The holiness which makes people think that "to put up with a saint you need two saints" is not true holiness. At best it would only be its caricature.

394 The devil tries to draw us away from God, and if you allow him to dominate you, good people will "draw away" from you, because they "draw away" from the devil's friends and from those possessed by him.

395 When you speak to God, even if you think yours are just empty words, ask him for a greater dedication, for a more determined progress towards Christian perfection. Ask him to put more fire into you!

396 Renew your firm resolution to live your Christian life *right now*, at every moment and in all circumstances.

397 Don't place obstacles in grace's way. You need to be convinced that in order to be leaven you must become a saint, and must struggle to identify yourself with Him.

398 Say slowly and in all earnestness: *Nunc coepi* – now I begin!

Don't get discouraged if, unfortunately, you don't see any great change in yourself brought about by the Lord's right hand... From your lowliness you can cry out: Help me, my Jesus, because I want to fulfil your Will... your most lovable Will!

399 Agreed: your concern ought to be for "them". But your first concern must be yourself, your own interior life. Otherwise, you will not be able to serve them.

400 How difficult you find that mortification suggested to you by the Holy Spirit! Look at a Crucifix, steadily... and you will come to love that expiation.

401 "To be nailed to the Cross!" This aspiration kept coming again and again, as a new light, to the mind and heart and lips of a certain soul.

"To be nailed to the Cross?", he asked himself. "How hard it is!" And yet he knew full well the way he had to go: *agere contra* – self-denial. This is why he earnestly implored, "Help me, Lord!"

402 Being at Calvary, where Jesus died, the experience of our own sins should move us to be sorry, to make a deeper and more mature decision not to offend him again.

403 We need to smooth off the rough edges a little more each day – just as if we were working in stone or wood – and get rid of the defects in our own lives with a spirit of penance. And with small mortifications, which are of two types: *active* mortifications – the ones we ourselves look for, like little flowers we gather up during the course of the day – and *passive* mortifications, which come from without and we find difficult to accept. Jesus Christ will later make up for whatever is still lacking.

–What a wonderful figure of the crucified Christ you will become if generously and cheerfully you give your all!

404 Our Lord, with his arms outstretched, is continually begging for your alms of love.

405 Draw close to Jesus who has died for you; draw close to that Cross, outlined against the sky on the summit of Golgotha...

But draw close sincerely and with interior recollection, which is the sign of Christian maturity. That way the divine and human events of the Passion will sink deep into your soul.

406 We should accept mortification with those same sentiments that Jesus Christ had in his Holy Passion.

407 Mortification is a necessary premise for any apostolate, and for the perfect carrying out of each apostolate.

408 A spirit of penance is to be found first of all in taking advantage of the many trifling occasions – deeds, renunciations, sacrifices, services rendered... – which we find daily along our way and we then convert into acts of love and contrition, into mortifications. In this way we shall be able to gather a bouquet at the end of each day – a fine bunch of flowers which we can offer to God!

409 The best spirit of sacrifice is to persevere in the work begun: when it is exciting and when it proves an uphill struggle.

410 Submit your plan of mortifications to your spiritual Director, for him to 'moderate' them.

–But to 'moderate' will not always mean to diminish. It can also mean increasing them, if he thinks fit. –Either way, accept his advice!

411 We can say with Saint Augustine that our evil passions tug at our garments, dragging us down. At the same time we are aware of great, noble and pure ambitions within our hearts, and know that a struggle is going on.

–If, with the grace of God, you make use of the ascetical means: if you seek to have presence of God, if you look for mortification and – don't be afraid – penance, then you will make progress, you will find peace and victory will be yours.

412 Custody of the heart. That priest used to pray: "Jesus, may my poor heart be an enclosed garden; may my poor heart be a paradise where you live; may my Guardian Angel watch over it with a sword of fire and use it to purify every affection before it comes into me. Jesus, with the divine seal of your Cross, seal my poor heart."

413 Each person in his own situation should lead a pure life, courageously lived. We have to learn to say *No* for the sake of that great Love, Love with a capital letter.

414 There is a Spanish saying which speaks clearly enough: *Entre santa y santo, pared de cal y canto* ("Twixt holy man and holy maid, a wall of solid stone be laid").

–We have to watch over our hearts and our senses, and pull ourselves away from all occasions of sin. No matter how holy it may appear, passion must not have its way!

415 Dear Lord, I find beauty and charm in everything I see! I will guard my sight at every moment, for the sake of Love.

416 You are a Christian and, as a Christian, a son of God. You should feel a grave responsibility for corresponding to the mercies you have received from the Lord, showing careful vigilance and loving firmness, so that nothing and nobody may disfigure the distinctive features of the Love he has imprinted on your soul.

417 You have reached a level of real intimacy with this God of ours, who is so close to you, so deeply lodged in your soul... But what are you doing to increase and deepen this intimacy? Are you careful not to allow silly little hindrances to creep in which would upset this friendship?

–Show courage! Don't refuse to break with every single thing, no matter how small, which could cause suffering to the One who loves you so much.

418 If we are faithful to him, Jesus' own life will somehow be repeated in the life of each one of us, both in its internal development (the process of sanctification) and in our outward behaviour.

–Give thanks to him for being so good.

419 It seems an excellent idea to me that you should tell the Lord often about your great and ardent desire to be a saint, even though you see yourself filled with wretchedness...

–Tell him, precisely because of this!

420 You have seen very clearly that you are a child of God. Even if you were never again to see it – it won't happen! – you should continue along your way forever, out of a sense of faithfulness, without ever looking back.

421 A resolution: to be faithful to my timetable – heroically faithful and without excuses – on ordinary days and on extra-ordinary days.

422 You might have thought occasionally, with holy envy, about the adolescent Apostle, John, *quem diligebat*

Iesus – whom Jesus loved.

–Wouldn't you like to deserve to be called "the one who loves the Will of God"? Then take the necessary steps, day after day.

423 You can be sure of the following: the desire – shown by deeds! – to live like a good son of God brings permanent youthfulness and serenity, joy and peace.

424 If you abandon yourself once more in God's hands, the Holy Spirit will give light to your understanding and strength to your will.

425 Listen to that parable which comes to us from Jesus' own lips and is told us by Saint John in his Gospel: *Ego sum vitis, vos palmites* – I am the vine, you are the branches.

Picture the whole parable in your imagination and in your mind. You will see that a branch separated from the stock, from the vine, is useless, it will not bear abundant fruit. It will end up like a dry stick which men or animals trample underfoot, or will be thrown on the fire...

–You are the branch; draw the necessary conclusions.

426 Today once again I prayed full of confidence. This was my petition: "Lord, may neither our past wretchedness which has been forgiven us, nor the possibility of future wretchedness cause us any disquiet. May we abandon ourselves into your merciful hands. May we bring before you our desires for sanctity and apostolate, which are hidden like embers under the ashes of an apparent coldness..."

–"Lord, I know you are listening to us." You should say this to him too.

427 Be sincere when you open up your soul. Speak out and don't try to sugar the pill; that could be a very childish thing to do.

And then continue on your way, with docility. You will be holier, and happier.

428 Don't look for consolations apart from God. – See what that priest wrote: There should be no unburdening of your heart to any other friend when there is no need to do so.

429 Holiness is attained with the help of the Holy Spirit, who comes to dwell in our souls, through grace given us by the sacraments and as a result of a constant ascetical struggle.

My son, let us not have any false illusions about this. You and I – I will never tire of repeating it – will always have to struggle, always, until the end of our lives. So we will come to love peace, and we will spread peace around us, and we will receive our everlasting reward.

430 Don't just talk to the Paraclete. Listen to him!

When you pray, consider how the life of childhood which enabled you to realise deeply that you are a son of God filled you with a filial love for the Father. Think how, before that, you have gone through Mary to Jesus, whom you adore as his friend, as his brother, as his lover for that is what you are...

After receiving this advice you realised that until now you had known that the Holy Spirit was dwelling in your soul, to sanctify it... But you hadn't really *grasped* this truth about his presence. You needed that advice. Now you feel his Love within you, and you want to talk to him, to be his friend, to confide in him... You want to facilitate his work of polishing, uprooting, and enkindling...

I wouldn't know how to set about it!, you thought. Listen to him, I insist. He will give you strength. He will do everything, if you so want... And you *do* want!

–Pray to him: Divine Guest, Master, Light, Guide, Love, may I make you truly welcome inside me and listen to the lessons you teach me. Make me burn with eagerness for you, make me follow you and love you.

431 To draw closer to God, to fly all the way to God, you need the strong and generous wings of Prayer and Expiation.

432 To avoid routine in your vocal prayers try to say them with the same ardour with which a person who has just fallen in love speaks... and as if it were the last chance you had to approach Our Lord.

433 If you feel proud to be a son of Our Lady, ask yourself: How often do I express my devotion to the Virgin Mary during the day, from morning to night?

434 There are two reasons, among others, that friend was saying to himself, why I should make reparation to my Immaculate Mother every Saturday and on the eve of her feasts.

The second is that on Sundays and on feasts of Our Lady (which are often feasts in villages), instead of dedicating such days to prayer, so many people spend them – you have only to look around you and see – offending Our Jesus with public sins and scandalous crimes.

The first reason is that, perhaps due to the devil's influence, those of us who want to be good sons are not taking proper care in the way we live these days dedicated to Our Lord and to his Mother.

You'll realise that unfortunately these reasons are still very valid. And so we too should make reparation.

435 I have always understood Christian

prayer as being a loving conversation with Jesus, which shouldn't be interrupted even in the moments when we are physically far from the Tabernacle, because our whole life is made up of verses of human love in a divine way ... and we can love always.

436 God's love for his creatures is so boundless and our response to it should be so great that, when Holy Mass is being said, time ought to stand still.

437 When the branches are united to the vine they grow to maturity and bear fruit.

–What then should you and I do? We should get right close to Jesus, through the Bread and through the Word. He is our vine... We should speak affectionate words to him throughout the day. That is what people in love do.

438 Love Our Lord very much. Maintain and foster in your soul a sense of urgency to love him better. Love God precisely now when perhaps a good many of those who hold him in their hands do not love him, but rather ill-treat and neglect him.

Be sure to take good care of the Lord for me, in the Holy Mass and throughout the whole day!

439 Prayer is the most powerful weapon a Christian has. Prayer makes us effective. Prayer makes us happy. Prayer gives us all the strength we need to fulfil God's commands.

–Yes!, your whole life can and should be prayer.

440 Personal sanctity is not an unrealistic idea, but a precise reality, which is both divine and human. And it manifests itself constantly in daily deeds of Love.

441 The spirit of prayer which fills the entire life of Jesus Christ among men teaches us that all our actions – great or small – ought to be preceded by prayer, accompanied by prayer and followed by prayer.

442 Contemplate and live the Passion of Christ, with Him. Proffer your own shoulders frequently, daily, when he is scourged; offer your own head to be crowned with thorns.

–Where I come from they say: "Love is repaid with love."

443 A person in love doesn't miss the tiniest detail. I have seen it in so many souls. Those little things become something very great: Love!

444 Love God for those who do not love him. You should make this spirit of reparation and atonement flesh of your flesh.

445 If at any time the going gets harder in our interior struggle, that will be a good moment to show that our Love is in earnest.

446 You are certain it was God who made you see quite clearly that you must return to the more childlike *little things* of your earlier interior life, and persevere for months and even years in those heroic trivialities. (You needn't take into account your feelings here since they are so often slow to recognise the good.) Your will may be cold but let it be ready to fulfil those little duties out of Love.

447 Persevere in your life of piety, willingly and with love, even if you feel arid. Don't worry if you find yourself counting the minutes or days still to go before you finish that act of piety or that job of work, with the turbid delight of the lazy schoolboy who in a similar situation is looking forward to the end of term; or of the petty criminal who can't wait to get back to his tricks once he is out of jail again.

Persevere, I insist, with a real and effective determination. Don't cease, not even for a moment, to want to fulfil and benefit from those means of piety.

448 Practise your faith cheerfully, keeping very close to Jesus Christ. Really love him – but really, really love him! – and you will take part in a great Adventure of Love, because you will be more in love each day.

449 Say slowly to the Master: Lord, all I want is to serve you. All I want is to fulfil my duties and love you with all my heart. Make me feel your firm step by my side. May you be my only support!

–Say this to him slowly... and really mean it!

450 You need interior life and doctrinal formation. Be demanding on yourself! As a Christian man or woman, you have to be the salt of the earth and the light of the world, for you are obliged to give good example with holy shamelessness.

The charity of Christ should compel you. Feeling and knowing yourself to be another Christ from the moment you told him that you would follow him, you must not separate yourself from your equals – your relatives, friends and colleagues – any more than you would separate salt from the food it is seasoning.

Your interior life and your formation include the piety and the principles a child of God must have, to give flavour to everything by his active presence there.

Ask the Lord that you may always be that good seasoning in the lives of others.

451 We Christians, with a spirit of youthfulness, have come to collect the treasures of the Gospels, which are always new, so that we can make them reach every corner of the earth.

452 You need to imitate Jesus Christ and make him known through your behaviour. I want you not to forget that Christ assumed our human nature so as to raise all men to a divine way of life; and so that, united to him, we might live the commands of Heaven both individually and as members of society.

453 You, being a Christian, cannot turn your back on any concern or need of other men, your brothers.

454 How very insistent the Apostle Saint John was in preaching the *mandatum novum*, the new commandment that we should love one another!

–I would fall on my knees, without putting on any act – but this is what my heart dictates – and ask you, for the love of God, to love one another, to help one another, to lend one another a hand, to know how to forgive one another.

–And so, reject all pride, be

compassionate, show charity; help each other with prayer and sincere friendship.

455 You will only be good if you know how to see the good points and the virtues of the others.

–That is why when you have to correct, you should do so with charity, at the opportune moment, without humiliating... And being ready yourself to learn and to improve in the very faults you are correcting.

456 Love and practise charity without setting any limits or discriminating between people, for it is the virtue which marks us out as disciples of the Master.

Nevertheless, this charity cannot lead you to dampen your faith – for it would then cease to be a virtue. Nor should it blur the clear outlines that define the faith, nor soften it to the point of changing it, as some people try to do, into something amorphous and lacking the strength and power of God.

457 You have to live in harmony with your fellow men and understand them as a brother would. As the Spanish mystic says, where there is no love, put love and you will find love.

458 Whenever you need to criticise, your criticism must seek to be positive, helpful and constructive. It should never be made behind the back of the person concerned.

–To act otherwise would be treacherous, sneaky, defamatory, slanderous perhaps..., and, always, utterly ignoble.

459 Whenever you see that the glory of God and the good of the Church demand that you should speak out, don't remain silent.

–Think about it. Who would lack courage before God and in the face of eternity? There is nothing to be lost and instead so much to be gained. Why do you hold back then?

460 We are not good brothers to our fellow men if we are not ready to continue behaving correctly, even when those around us may interpret our actions badly or react in an unpleasant manner.

461 Your love for Mother Church and the service you render her should in no way be conditioned by the greater or lesser holiness of the individuals who make up the Church, even though we ardently desire that everyone will achieve Christian perfection.

–You have to love the Spouse of Christ, your Mother. She is, and always will be, pure and spotless.

462 Our striving for our own sanctification has repercussions on the sanctity of so many souls and also on the sanctity of God's Church.

463 Be convinced of this!: if only you wish it (and don't forget that God listens to you and loves you and promises you glory and you will be protected by the almighty hand of your Father in Heaven) you can be a person full of fortitude, ready to be a witness everywhere to the most lovable truth of his doctrine.

464 The Lord's field is fertile and the seed he sows of good quality. Therefore when weeds appear in this world of ours, never doubt that they spring up because of a lack of correspondence on the part of men, Christians especially, who have fallen asleep and have left the field open to the enemy.

–Don't complain, for there's no point; examine your behaviour, instead.

465 The following comment, which caused me great sorrow, will also make you reflect: "I see very clearly why there is a lack of resistance, and why what resistance there is to iniquitous laws is so ineffective, for above, below and in the middle there are many people – so very many! – who just follow the crowd."

466 The enemies of God and of his Church, manipulated by the devil's unremitting hatred, are relentless in their activities and organization.

With "exemplary" constancy they prepare their cadres, run schools, appoint leaders and deploy agitators. In an undercover way – but very effectively – they spread their ideas and sow, in homes and places of work, a seed which is destructive of any religious ideology.

–What is there that we Christians should not be ready to do, always with the truth, to serve our God?

467 Don't confuse serenity with laziness, with neglect, and putting off making decisions or studying questions that need attending to.

Serenity always goes hand in hand with diligence, which is a virtue we need in order to consider and resolve pending matters without delay.

468 –My son, where is the Christ that people look for in you? ? In your pride? In your desire to impose yourself on others? In those defects of character which you don't wish to overcome? In your stubbornness?... Is Christ to be found there? No, he is not!

–You need to have your own personality, agreed. But you should try to make it conform exactly to Christ's.

469 I will suggest to you a good rule of conduct for living fraternity and a spirit of service. When you are not around, other people should be able to go ahead with the work you have in hand thanks to the experience you have generously passed on to them, and to your not having made yourself indispensable.

470 It is you – in spite of your passions – who have the responsibility over the sanctity of the others, for their Christian behaviour and for their effectiveness.

You are not on your own. If you stop you could be holding up or harming so many people!

471 Think about your Mother the Holy Church and consider how, if one member suffers, the whole body suffers.

–Your body needs each one of its members, but each member needs the whole body. What would happen if my hands were to stop doing their duty... or if my heart were to stop beating!

472 You saw it quite clearly: while so

many people do not know God, he has looked to you. He wants you to form a foundation stone, an ashlar, on which the life of the Church can rest.

Meditate on this reality and you will draw many practical consequences for your ordinary behaviour: the foundation stone – hidden and possibly rather dull – has to be solid, showing no weakness. It has to serve as a support for the building... If not, it remains isolated.

473 Since you feel you have been chosen by God to support and co-redeem – without forgetting that you are... wretched and utterly so – your humility should lead you to place yourself under the feet – at the service – of all. This is what the supports of a building do.

But foundations need to be strong. Fortitude is an indispensable virtue for someone who has to sustain or encourage others.

–Say this to Jesus and say it to him strongly: May I never through false humility stop practising the cardinal virtue of fortitude. Make me know how to separate, my God, the gold from the dross.

474 Our Mother, our Hope! How safe and sure we are when we keep nice and close to you, even when everything around us is quivering and shaking.

RECOVERY

475 You feel the need of conversion: He is asking more of you... and you are giving him less each day!

476 For each one of us, as for Lazarus, it was really a *veni foras* – come out – which got us moving.

–How sad it is to see those who are still dead and don't know the power of God's mercy!

–Renew your holy joy, for opposite the man who is decomposing without Christ, there is another who has risen with him.

477 Earthly affections, even when they aren't just squalid concupiscence, usually involve some element of selfishness.

So, though you must not despise those affections – they can be very holy – always make sure you purify your intention.

478 Don't be anxious for people to sympathise with you. That is often a sign of pride or vanity.

479 Whenever you speak of the theological virtues, of faith, of hope, of love, remember that, rather than to theorise on, they are virtues to be practised.

480 Is there something in your life that does not suit your dignity as a Christian, something which makes you unwilling to be cleansed?

–Examine your conscience, and change.

481 Take a good look at the way you behave. You will see that you are full of faults that harm you and perhaps also those around you.

–Remember, my child, that microbes may be no less a menace than wild beasts. And you are cultivating those errors and those mistakes – just as bacteria are cultivated in a laboratory – with your lack of humility, with your lack of prayer, with your failure to fulfil your duty, with your lack of self-knowledge... Those tiny germs then spread everywhere.

–You need to make a good examination of conscience every day. It will lead you to make definite resolutions to improve, because it will have made you really sorry for your shortcomings, omissions and sins.

482 Almighty God, Omnipotent and Infinitely Wise, had to choose his Mother.

What would you have done, if you had had to choose yours? I think that you and I would have chosen the mother we have, filling her with all graces. That is what God did: and that is why, after the Blessed Trinity, comes Mary.

–Theologians have given a rational explanation for her fullness of grace and why she cannot be subject to the devil: it was fitting that it should be so, God could do it, therefore he did it. That is the great proof: the clearest proof that God endowed his Mother with every privilege, from the very first moment. That is how she is: beautiful, and pure, and spotless in soul and body!

483 You are expecting victory, the end of the struggle... but it doesn't come?

–Thank God, as if you had already reached that goal, and offer him your feelings of impatience: *Vir fidelis loquetur victoriam*, the faithful man will sing the joys of victory.

484 There are moments in which you are deprived of that union with Our Lord which enabled you to pray continually, even when you were asleep. You seem almost to be wrestling with God's Will.

–It is weakness, as you well know. Love the Cross, love the lack of so many things which everyone thinks necessary, the obstacles as you start or... as you go along on your way, your very littleness and spiritual wretchedness.

–Offer – with a desire that is effective – all you have, and all that belongs to those who are yours. Humanly speaking, it's quite a lot, but from a supernatural point of view, it's nothing.

485 At times, someone has told me: "Father, I feel tired and cold; when I pray or fulfil some other norm of piety, I seem to be acting out a farce..."

To that friend, and to you, if you are in the same boat, I answer: A farce? –What an excellent thing, my child! Act out that farce! The Lord is your audience – the Father, the Son, and the Holy Spirit. The Blessed Trinity is contemplating us in those moments when we are "acting out a farce".

Acting like that in front of God, out of love, in order to please him, when our whole life goes against the grain: how splendid, to be God's juggler! How marvellous it is to play one's part for Love, with sacrifice, without any personal satisfaction, just in order to please Our Lord!

–That indeed is to live for Love.

486 A heart which loves the things of the earth beyond measure is like one fastened by a chain – or by a " fine thread" – which stops it flying to God.

487 "Watch and pray, that you may not enter into temptation..." It makes one shudder to see how someone can give up a divine undertaking for the sake of a fleeting delusion!

488 A lukewarm apostle: that's the great enemy of souls.

489 A clear sign of lukewarmness is a lack of supernatural "stubbornness", of fortitude to keep on working and not stop until you have laid "the last stone".

490 Some hearts are hard, but noble. When they come close to the warmth of Christ's Heart, they melt like bronze into tears of love, of reparation. They catch fire.

But lukewarm people have hearts of clay, of mean flesh... They crack and turn to dust. A sorry sight.

Say with me: "Our Jesus, keep us from being lukewarm. We do not want to be lukewarm!"

491 All goodness, all beauty, all majesty, all loveliness, all grace adorn our Mother. –Doesn't it make you fall in love, to have a Mother like that?

492 We are in love with Love. That is why Our Lord doesn't want us to be dry, stiff, lifeless. He wants us to be steeped in his tenderness!

493 See if you can understand this apparent contradiction. At thirty years of age, that man wrote in his diary: "I'm not young any more." When he was over forty, he wrote again: "I will stay young till I'm eighty: if I die before that, I'll think I haven't done my stint."

–Wherever he went he took with him, in spite of the passing years, the mature youthfulness of Love.

494 How well I understand that question put by a soul in love with God: "Have I made any grimace of distaste, has there been anything in me which could, my Lord, my Love, have hurt you?"

–Ask your Father-God to grant us that constant requirement to love.

495 Have you seen the affection and the confidence with which Christ's friends treat him? In a completely natural way the sisters of Lazarus reproach Jesus for being away: "We told you! If only you'd been here!..."

–Speak to him with calm confidence: "Teach me to treat you with the loving friendliness of Martha, Mary and Lazarus and as the first Twelve treated you, even though at first they followed you perhaps for not very supernatural reasons."

496 What a pleasure it is to contemplate John, leaning his head on Christ's breast! –It is like giving up one's intelligence lovingly, difficult though this is, to let it be set on fire by the flame of the Heart of Jesus.

497 God loves me... And John the Apostle writes: "Let us love God, then, since God loved us first."–As if this were not enough, Jesus comes to each one of us, in spite of our patent wretchedness, to ask us, as he asked Peter: "Simon, son of John, do you love me more than these others?..."

–This is the moment to reply: "Lord, you know all things, you know that I love you!" adding, with humility, "Help me to love you more. Increase my love!"

498 "Love means deeds and not sweet words." Deeds, deeds! And a resolution: I will continue to tell you very often that I love you. How often have I repeated this today! But, with your grace, it will be my behaviour above all that shows it. It will be the little things of each day which, with silent eloquence, will cry out before you, showing you my Love.

499 We men don't know how to show Jesus the gentle refinements of love that some poor, rough fellows – Christians all the same – show daily to some pitiful little creature (their wife, their child, their friend) who is as poor as they.

–This truth should serve as a salutary shock to make us react.

500 The Love of God is so attractive, and so fascinating, that there are no limits to its growth in the life of a Christian.

501 You cannot behave like a naughty child, or like a madman.

–You have to be strong, a child of God. You have to be calm in your professional work and in your dealings with others, with a presence of God which makes you give perfect attention to even the smallest details.

502 If bare justice is done, people may feel hurt.

–Always act, therefore, for the love of God, which will add to that justice the balm of a neighbourly love, and will purify and cleanse all earthly love.

When you bring God in, everything becomes supernatural.

503 Love Our Lord passionately. Love him madly! Because if there is love there – when there is love – I would dare to say that resolutions are not needed. My parents – think of yours – did not need to make any resolutions to love me: and what an effusion of tenderness they showed me, in little details every day!

With that same human heart we can and should love God.

504 Love is sacrifice; and sacrifice for Love's sake is a joy.

505 Answer this question in your heart: How often each day does your will ask you to set your heart on God, to give him your expressions of love and your actions?

This is a good way to measure the intensity and quality of your love.

506 Be convinced, my child, that God has a right to ask us: Are you thinking about me? Are you aware of me? Do you look to me as your support? Do you seek me as the Light of your life, as your shield..., as your all?

–Renew, then, this resolution: In times the world calls good I will cry out: "Lord!" In times it calls bad, again I will cry: "Lord!"

507 I don't want you ever to lose your supernatural outlook. Even though you see your own meannesses, your evil inclinations – the clay of which you are made – in all their raw shamefulness, God is counting on you.

508 Live as the others around you live, with naturalness, but "supernaturalising" every moment of your day.

509 To be able to judge with rectitude of intention what is needed is a pure heart, zeal for the things of God and love of souls, free from prejudices.

–Think about it!

510 I heard some people I knew talking about their radio sets. Almost without realising it, I brought the subject round to the spiritual area: we have got a strong earth, too strong, and we have forgotten to put up the aerial of the interior life...

–That is why there are so few souls who keep in touch with God. May we never be without our supernatural aerial.

511 Do trifles and trivialities, that bring me nothing and from which I expect nothing, engage my attention more than my God? Who am I with, when I am not with God?

512 Tell him: Lord, I want nothing other than what You want. Even those things I am asking you for at present, if they take me a millimetre away from your Will, don't give them to me.

513 The secret of being effective, at root, lies in your piety, a sincere piety. This way you will pass the whole day with Him.

514 A resolution: to "keep up", without interruption as far as you can, a loving and docile friendship and conversation with the Holy Spirit. *Veni, Sancte Spiritus...!* – Come, O Holy Spirit, and dwell in my soul!

515 Repeat to yourself, with all your heart, and with ever-increasing love, and more when you are in front of the Tabernacle or have the Lord within your breast: *Non est qui se abscondat a calore eius* – "No one can hide from his warmth." May I not flee from you, may I be filled with the fire of your Holy Spirit.

516 *Ure igne Sancti Spiritus!* – burn me with the fire of your Spirit, you cried. You then added: "My poor soul needs to fly again as soon as possible..., and not stop flying until it rests in God!"

–I think your desires are admirable. I will pray for you often to the Paraclete. I will invoke him continually, so that he may nestle in the centre of your being, presiding and giving a supernatural tone to all your actions and words, thoughts and desires.

517 When you celebrated the feast of the Exaltation of the Holy Cross you asked Our Lord, with the most earnest desire of your heart, to grant you his grace so as to "exalt" the Holy Cross in the powers of your soul and in your senses... You asked for a new life; for the Cross to set a seal on it, to confirm the truth of your mission; for the whole of your being to rest on the Cross!
–We shall see...

518 Mortification has to be constant, like the beating of the heart. In this way we will have dominion over ourselves and the charity of Christ for others.

519 To love the Cross means being able to put oneself out, gladly, for the love of Christ, though it's hard – and because it's hard. You have enough experience to know that this is not a contradiction.

520 Christian cheerfulness is not something physiological. Its foundation is supernatural, and it goes deeper than illness or difficulties.

–Cheerfulness does not mean the jingling of bells, or the gaiety of a dance at the local hall.

True cheerfulness is something deeper, something within: something that keeps us peaceful and brimming over with joy, though at times our face may be stern.

521 I wrote to you: Though I can understand that it's not an uncommon way of talking, I'm not happy when I hear people describe the difficulties born of pride as "crosses". These burdens are not the Cross, the true Cross, because they are not Christ's Cross.

So struggle against those invented obstacles, which have nothing to do with the seal Christ has set on you. Get rid of all the disguises of self!

522 Even on those days when you seem to be wasting time, in the prose of the thousand details of the day there is more than enough poetry for you to feel that you are on the Cross: on a Cross which no one notices.

523 Do not fix your heart on anything that passes away. Imitate Christ, who became poor for us, and had nowhere to lay his head.

–Ask him to give you, in the midst of the world, a real detachment, a detachment that has nothing to soften it.

524 One clear sign of detachment is genuinely not to consider anything as one's own.

525 Whoever really lives his faith knows that the goods of the world are means, and uses them generously, heroically.

526 The risen Christ, Christ in glory, has divested himself of the things of this earth, so that we men, his brothers, should ask ourselves what things we need to get rid of.

527 We have to love the Blessed Virgin Mary more. We will never love her enough!

–Love her a lot! It shouldn't be enough

for you to put up pictures of her, and greet them, and say aspirations. You should learn to offer her, in your strenuous life, some small sacrifice each day, to show her your love, and to show her the kind of love that we want the whole human race to proclaim for her.

528 This is the truth of a Christian's life: self-giving and love – love of God and, for God's sake, love of one's neighbour – founded on sacrifice.

529 Jesus, I put myself trustingly in Your arms, hiding my head on Your loving breast, my heart touching Yours: I want what You want, in everything.

530 Nowadays the world we live in is full of disobedience and gossip, of intrigue and conspiracy. So, more than ever we have to love obedience, sincerity, loyalty and simplicity: and all this with a supernatural outlook, which will make us more human.

531 You say yes, you are determined to follow Christ.

–All right. Then you should walk at his pace, not at your own!

532 You want to know on what our faithfulness is founded?

–I would say, in broad outline, that it is based on loving God, which makes us overcome all kinds of obstacles: selfishness, pride, tiredness, impatience...

–A man in love tramples on his own self. He is aware that even when he is loving with all his soul, he doesn't yet know how to love enough.

533 I was told – and I write it down, because it's very beautiful – about the way of speaking of a goodly nun from Aragon, in her gratitude for God's fatherly goodness: "How 'smart' he is! He's got his eye on everything."

534 You too, like all God's children, need personal prayer. You need to be intimate with him, to talk directly with Our Lord. You need a two-way conversation, face to face, without hiding yourself in anonymity.

535 The first thing needed in prayer is perseverance the second, humility.

–Have a holy stubbornness, be trusting. Remember that when we ask the Lord for something important, he may want to be asked for many years. Keep on! But keep on with ever increasing trust.

536 Persevere in prayer, as the Master told us. This point of departure will be your source of peace, of cheerfulness, of serenity, and so it will make you humanly and supernaturally effective.

537 You were in a place where they were talking and listening to music. Prayer welled up in your soul, bringing an unspeakable solace. In the end you said: "Jesus, I don't want consolation; I want you."

538 Your life must be a constant prayer, a never-ceasing conversation with Our Lord: when things are pleasant or unpleasant, easy or difficult, usual or unusual...

In every situation, your conversation with your Father God should immediately come to life. You should seek him right within your soul.

539 To recollect oneself in prayer, in meditation, is so easy! Jesus doesn't make us wait. He doesn't leave us in the waiting-room. It is he who does the waiting.

You only have to say "Lord, I want to pray, I want to talk to you!" and you are at once in God's presence, talking to him.

And as if this were not enough, he doesn't begrudge you his time. He leaves it up to you, just as you please. And not just for ten minutes or a quarter of an hour, but for hours and hours! For the whole day! And he is who he is: the Almighty, the Most Wise.

540 In the interior life, as in human love, we have to persevere.

Yes, you have to meditate often on the same themes, keeping on until you re-discover an old discovery.

–"And how could I not have seen this so clearly before?" you'll ask in surprise. Simply because sometimes we're like stones, that let the water flow over them, without absorbing a drop.

–That's why we have to go over the same things again and again – because they aren't the same things – if we want to soak up God's blessings.

541 In the Holy Sacrifice of the altar, the priest takes up the Body of our God, and the Chalice containing his Blood, and raises them above all the things of the earth, saying: *Per Ipsum, et cum Ipso, et in Ipso* – through My Love, with My Love, in My Love!

Unite yourself to the action of the priest. Or rather, make that reality a part of your life.

542 The Gospel tells us that Jesus, after he had worked the miracle, when they wanted to crown him king, hid himself.

–Lord, you make us share in the miracle of the Eucharist. We beg you not to hide away. Live with us. May we see you, may we touch you, may we feel you. May we want to be beside you all the time, and have you as the King of our lives and of our work.

543 Talk to the Three Persons, to God the Father, to God the Son, to God the Holy Spirit. And so as to reach the Blessed Trinity, go through Mary.

544 You don't have *living* faith if you aren't giving yourself to Jesus here and now.

545 All Christians should seek Christ and get to know him, so as to love him better and better. It's like courting. A couple need to get to know each other well, for if they don't, they will not really love each other. And our life is a life of Love.

546 Pause to consider the holy wrath of the Master, when he sees that the things of his Father are badly treated in the Temple at Jerusalem.

–What a lesson for you! You should never be indifferent, or play the coward, when the things of God are treated without respect.

547 Fall in love with the Sacred Humanity of Jesus Christ.

–Aren't you glad that he should have

wanted to be like us? Thank Jesus for this wonderful expression of his goodness!

548 Advent is here. What a marvellous time in which to renew your desire, your nostalgia, your real longing for Christ to come – for him to come every day to your soul in the Eucharist. The Church encourages us: *Ecce veniet!* – He is about to arrive!

549 Christmas. The carols sing *Venite, venite*, "O come ye, O come ye." Let us go to him. He has just been born.

After contemplating how Mary and Joseph care for the Child, I now dare to hint to you: Look at him again, gaze at him without ceasing.

550 Although it pains us to admit it – and I ask God to increase that sorrow in us – you and I have our share in the death of Christ. For the sins of men were the hammer-blows which stitched him to the Cross with nails.

551 Saint Joseph: One cannot love Jesus and Mary without loving the Holy Patriarch.

552 There are many good reasons to honour Saint Joseph, and to learn from his life. He was a man of strong faith. He earned a living for his family – Jesus and Mary – with his own hard work... He guarded the purity of the Blessed Virgin, who was his Spouse. And he respected – he loved! – God's freedom, when God made his choice: not only his choice of Our Lady the Virgin as his Mother, but also his choice of Saint Joseph as the Husband of Holy Mary.

553 Saint Joseph, our Father and Lord: most chaste, most pure. You were found worthy to carry the Child Jesus in your arms, to wash him, to hug him. Teach us to get to know God, and to be pure, worthy of being other Christs.

And help us to do and to teach, as Christ did. Help us to open up the divine paths of the earth, which are both hidden and bright; and help us to show them to mankind, telling our fellow men that their lives on earth can have an extraordinary and constant supernatural effectiveness.

554 Love Saint Joseph a lot. Love him with all your soul, because he, together with Jesus, is the person who has most loved our Blessed Lady and been closest to God. He is the person who has most loved God, after our Mother.

–He deserves your affection, and it will do you good to get to know him, because he is the Master of the interior life, and has great power before the Lord and before the Mother of God.

555 Our Lady. Who could be a better Teacher of the love of God than this Queen, this Lady, this Mother, who has the closest bond with the Trinity: Daughter of God the Father, Mother of God the Son, Spouse of God the Holy Spirit? And at the same time she is our Mother!

–Go and pray personally for her intercession.

556 You will become a saint if you have charity, if you manage to do the things which please others and do not offend God, though you find them hard to do.

557 Saint Paul has given us a wonderful recipe for charity: *alter alterius onera portate et sic adimplebitis legem Christi* – bear one another's burdens, and so you will fulfil the law of Christ.

–Is this what happens in your life?

558 Jesus Our Lord loved men so much that he became incarnate, took to himself our nature, and lived in daily contact with the poor and the rich, with the just and with sinners, with young and old, with Gentiles and Jews.

He spoke constantly to everyone: to those who showed good will towards him, and to those who were only looking for a way to twist his words and condemn him.

–You should try to act as Our Lord did.

559 Loving souls for God's sake will make us love everyone: understanding, excusing, forgiving...

We should have a love that can cover the multitude of failings contrived by human wretchedness. We have to have a wonderful charity, *veritatem facientes in caritate*, defending the truth, without hurting anyone.

560 When I speak to you of good example, I mean to tell you, too, that you have to understand and excuse, that you have to fill the world with peace and love.

561 Ask yourself often: am I making a real effort to be more refined in my charity towards the people I live with?

562 When I preach that we have to make ourselves a carpet so that the others may tread softly, I am not simply being poetic: it has to be a reality!

–It's hard, as sanctity is hard; but it's also easy, because, I insist, sanctity is within everyone's reach.

563 In the midst of so much selfishness, so much coldness –everyone out for what he can get – I call to mind those little wooden donkeys. They were trotting on a desk-top, strong and sturdy. One had lost a leg, but it carried on forward, supported by the others.

564 When we Catholics defend and uphold the truth, without making concessions, we have to strive to create an atmosphere of charity, of harmony, to drown all hatred and resentment.

565 In a Christian, in a child of God, friendship and charity are one and the same thing. They are a divine light which spreads warmth.

566 To practise fraternal correction – which is so deeply rooted in the Gospel – is a proof of supernatural trust and affection.

Be thankful for it when you receive it, and don't neglect to practise it with those you live with.

567 When you correct someone – because it has to be done and you want to do your duty – you must expect to hurt others and to get hurt yourself.

But you should never let this fact be an excuse for holding back.

568 Get very close to your Mother, the Virgin Mary. You ought to be united to God always: seek that union with him by staying near his Blessed Mother.

569 Listen to me: being in the world and belonging to the world does not mean being worldly.

570 You have to act like a burning coal, spreading fire wherever it happens to be; or at least, striving to raise the spiritual temperature of the people around you, leading them to live a truly Christian life.

571 God wants the works he entrusts to men to go ahead on the basis of prayer and mortification.

572 The foundation of all we do as citizens – as Catholic citizens – lies in an intense interior life. It lies in being really and truly men and women who turn their day into an uninterrupted conversation with God.

573 When you are with someone, you have to see a soul: a soul who has to be helped, who has to be understood, with whom you have to live in harmony, and who has to be saved.

574 You insist on trying to walk on

your own, doing your own will, guided solely by your own judgement... And you can see for yourself that the fruit of this is *fruitlessness*.

My child, if you don't give up your own judgement, if you are proud, if you devote yourself to "your" apostolate, you will work all night – your whole life will be one long night –and at the end of it all the dawn will find you with your nets empty.

575 To think of Christ's Death means to be invited to face up to our everyday tasks with complete sincerity, and to take the faith that we profess seriously.

It has to be an opportunity to go deeper into the depths of God's Love, so as to be able to show that Love to men with our words and deeds.

576 Make sure that your lips, the lips of a Christian – for that is what you are and should be at all times – speak those *compelling* supernatural words which will move and encourage, and will show your committed attitude to life.

577 There is a great love of comfort, and at times a great irresponsibility, hidden behind the attitude of those in authority who flee from the sorrow of correcting, making the excuse that they want to avoid the suffering of others.

They may perhaps save themselves some discomfort in this life. But they are gambling with eternal happiness – the eternal happiness of others as well as their own – by these omissions of theirs. These omissions are real sins.

578 For many people a saint is an "uncomfortable" person to live with. But this doesn't mean that he has to be unbearable.

–A saint's zeal should never be bitter. When he corrects he should never be wounding. His example should never be an arrogant moral slap in his neighbour's face.

579 There was a young priest who used to address Jesus with the words of the Apostles: *Edissere nobis parabolam*, explain the parable to us. He would add: Master, put into our souls the clarity of your teaching, so that it may never be absent from our lives and our works. And so that we can give it to others.

–You too should say this to Our Lord.

580 Always have the courage – the humility, the desire to serve God – to put forward the truths of faith as they are, not allowing any concessions, nor ambiguities.

581 There is no other possible attitude for a Catholic: we have to defend the authority of the Pope *always*, and to be ready *always* to correct our own views with docility, in line with the teaching authority of the Church.

582 A long time ago someone asked me, tactlessly, whether those of us whose career is the priesthood are able to retire when we get old. And since I gave him no answer, he persisted with his impertinent question.

–Then an answer came to me which, I thought, is indisputable. "The priesthood", I told him, "is not a career: it is an apostolate."

–That's how I feel about it. And I wanted to put it down in these notes so that

– with God's help – none of us may ever forget the difference.

583 To have a Catholic spirit means that we should feel on our shoulders the weight of our concern for the entire Church – not just of this or that particular part of it. It means that our prayer should spread out north and south, east and west, in a generous act of petition.

So you will understand the cry – the aspiration – of that friend of ours, faced by the little love of so many people towards our Holy Mother: "I suffer for my Church!"

584 "There is the daily pressure upon me of my anxiety for all the churches", Saint Paul wrote. This sigh of the Apostle is a reminder for all Christians – for you, too – of our responsibility to place at the feet of the Spouse of Christ, of the Holy Church, all that we are and all that we can do; loving her most faithfully, even at the cost of livelihood, of honour, of life itself.

585 Don't be scared by it. In so far as you can you should fight against the conspiracy of silence they want to muzzle the Church with. Some people stop her voice being heard; others will not let the good example of those who preach with their deeds be seen; others wipe out every trace of good doctrine..., and so very many cannot bear to hear her.

Don't be scared, I say again. But don't get tired, either, of your task of being a loud-speaker for the teachings of the Magisterium.

586 Become more *Roman* day by day. Love that blessed quality which is the ornament of the children of the one true Church, for Jesus wanted it to be so.

587 Devotion to Our Lady in Christian souls awakens the supernatural stimulus we need, to act like *domestici Dei*, as members of God's family.

VICTORY

588 Imitate the Blessed Virgin. Only by fully admitting that we are nothing can we become precious in the eyes of our Creator.

589 I am convinced that John, the young Apostle, is at the side of Christ on the Cross because our Mother draws him there. The Love of Our Lady is so powerful!

590 We will never achieve true supernatural and human cheerfulness, *real* good humour, if we don't *really* imitate Jesus: if we aren't humble, as he was.

591 To give oneself sincerely to others is so effective that God rewards it with a humility filled with cheerfulness.

592 Our humiliation, our self-effacement, our disappearing and passing unnoticed, should be complete, entire, total.

593 Sincere humility. What can upset a person who delights in being insulted because he knows that he deserves nothing better?

594 My Jesus: what's mine is yours, because what's yours is mine, and what's mine I abandon in you.

595 Are you able to undergo those humiliations which God asks of you, in matters of no importance, matters where the truth is not obscured? You are not? Then you don't love the virtue of humility.

596 Pride dulls the edge of charity. Ask Our Lord each day for the virtue of humility, for you and for everyone. Because as the years go by, pride increases if it is not corrected in time.

597 Is there anything more displeasing than a child acting the grown-up? How can a poor man – a child – be pleasing to God if he "acts grown-up", puffed up by pride, sure that he's worth something and trusting only in himself?

598 Certainly you can go to Hell. You are convinced it could happen, for in your heart you find the seeds of all kinds of evil.

But if you become a child in front of God, that fact will bring you close to your Father God, and to your Mother, Holy Mary. And Saint Joseph and your Angel will not leave you unprotected when they see you are a child.

–Have faith. Do as much as you can. Be penitent, and be Loving! They will supply whatever else you need.

599 How difficult it is to live humility! As the popular wisdom of Christianity says, "Pride dies twenty-four hours after its owner."

So when you think you're right, against what you are being told by someone who has been given a special grace from God to guide your soul, be sure that you are *completely wrong*.

600 Serving and forming children, caring lovingly for the sick.

To make ourselves understood by simple souls, we have to humble our intelligence; to understand poor sick people we have to humble our heart. In this way, on our knees in both intellect and body, it is easy to reach Jesus along that sure way of human wretchedness, of our own wretchedness. It will lead us to make 'a nothing' of ourselves in order to let God build on our nothingness.

601 A resolution: unless I really have to, never to speak of my personal affairs.

602 Thank Jesus for the confidence he gives you! It's not stubbornness, but God's light that makes you firm as a rock. Meanwhile, others, good as they are, present a sorry picture. They seem to be sinking in the sand... They lack the foundation of the faith.

Ask Our Lord to grant that the demands of the virtue of faith may be met both in your life and in the lives of others.

603 If I behaved differently, if I were more in control of my character, if I were more faithful to you, Lord, how marvellously would you help us!

604 The longing for atonement that your Father God puts in your soul will be satisfied if you unite your poor personal expiation to the infinite merits of Jesus.

–Rectify your intention, and love suffering in him, with him, and through him.

605 You don't know whether you are making progress, nor how much... But what use is such a reckoning to you?...

–What is important is that you should persevere, that your heart should be on fire, that you should be more enlightened and descry farther horizons; that you should strive for our intentions, that you should feel them as your own – even though you don't know what they are – and that you should pray for all of them.

606 Tell him: Jesus, I cannot see a single perfect flower in my garden, all are blighted. It seems that all have lost their colour and their scent. Poor me! Face downwards in the muck, on the ground: that's my place.

–That's the way, humble yourself. He will conquer in you, and you will attain the victory.

607 I understood you very well when you ended up saying: "Quite honestly, I haven't even made the grade of being a donkey – the donkey that was the throne of Jesus when he entered Jerusalem. I'm just part of a disgusting heap of dirty tatters that the poorest rag-picker would ignore."

But I told you: all the same, God has chosen you and wants you to be his instrument. So your wretchedness – which is a genuine fact – should turn into one more reason for you to be thankful to God for calling you.

608 Mary's humble song of joy, the *Magnificat*, recalls to our minds the infinite generosity of the Lord towards those who become like children, towards those who abase themselves and are sincerely aware that they are nothing.

609 God is very pleased with those who recognise his goodness by reciting the *Te Deum* in thanksgiving whenever something out of the ordinary happens, without caring whether it may have been good or bad, as the world reckons these things. Because everything comes from the hands of our Father: so though the blow of the chisel may hurt our flesh, it is a sign of Love, as he smooths off our rough edges and brings us closer to perfection.

610 When human beings have work to do they try to use the right tools for the job.

If I had lived in another century, I would have written with a quill pen: now I use a fountain pen.

But when God wants to carry out some piece of work, he uses unsuitable means, so that it can be seen that the work is his. How often you have heard me say this!

So you and I, who are aware of the massive weight of our failings, should tell Our Lord: "Wretched as I am, I still understand that in your hands I am a divine instrument."

611 We will dedicate all the exertions of our life, great and small, to the honour of God the Father, God the Son, and God the Holy Spirit.

–I am moved when I recall the work of those brilliant professionals – two engineers and two architects – cheerfully moving furniture into a student residence. When they had put a blackboard into a classroom, the first thing those four artists wrote was: *Deo omnis gloria!* – all the glory to God.

–Jesus, I know that this pleased you greatly.

612 Wherever you may happen to be, remember that the Son of Man did not come to be served, but to serve. Be sure that anyone who wants to follow him cannot attempt to act in any other way.

613 God has a special right over us, his children: it is the right to our response to his love, in spite of our failings. This inescapable truth puts us under an obligation which we cannot shirk. But it also gives us complete confidence: we are instruments in the hands of God, instruments that he relies on every day. That is why, every day, we struggle to serve him.

614 God expects his instruments to do what they can to be fit and ready: you should strive to make sure you are always fit and ready.

615 I have come to see that every Hail Mary, every greeting to Our Lady, is a new beat of a heart in love.

616 Our life – a Christian's life – has to be as ordinary as this: trying every day to do well those very things it is our duty to do; carrying out our divine mission in the world by fulfilling the little duty of each moment.

–Or rather, struggling to fulfil it. Sometimes we don't manage, and when night comes, in our examination, we'll have to tell Our Lord, "I am not offering you virtues; today I can only offer you defects. But with your grace I will be able to count myself a victor."

617 I wish with all my heart that God, in his mercy, in spite of your sins (may you never offend Jesus again!), may make you "constantly live that blessed life which is to love his Will".

618 In God's service there are no unimportant posts: all are of great importance.

–The importance of the post depends on the spiritual level reached by the person filling it.

619 Aren't you glad to have the sure confidence that God is interested in even the tiniest details of his creatures?

620 Show him again that you really want to be his. "O Jesus, help me. Make me really yours; may I burn and be consumed, by dint of little things that no one notices."

621 The Holy Rosary: the joys, the sorrows, and the glories of the life of Our Lady weave a crown of praises, repeated ceaselessly by the Angels and the Saints in Heaven – and by those who love our Mother here on earth.

–Practise this holy devotion every day, and spread it.

622 Baptism makes us *fideles*, faithful. This is a word that was used – like *sancti*, the saints – by the first followers of Jesus to refer to one another. These words are still used today: we speak of *the faithful* of the Church.

–Think about this.

623 God does not let himself be outdone in generosity. Be very sure that he grants faithfulness to those who give themselves to him.

624 Don't be afraid to be demanding on yourself. Many souls do so in their hidden life, so that only Jesus may shine out.

I wish you and I would react as that person did who wanted to be very close to God, on the feast of the Holy Family. In those days it was celebrated within the octave of the Epiphany.

–"I have had a number of little crosses. There was one yesterday that hurt so much it made me weep. Today it made me think that my Father and Lord Saint Joseph, and my Mother, Holy Mary, won't have left this child of theirs without its Christmas present. The present was the light that made me see my thanklessness to Jesus in my failing to correspond to his grace; and to see how mistaken I was to resist, by my boorish behaviour, the most Holy Will of God, who wants me as his instrument."

625 When the holy women reached the tomb, they found that the stone had been rolled aside.

This is what always happens! When we make up our minds to do what we should, the difficulties are easily overcome.

626 Be convinced that if you do not learn to obey you will never be effective.

627 When you are told what to do, let no one show more alacrity than you in obeying; whether it is hot or cold, whether you feel keen or are tired, whether you are young or less so, it makes no odds.

Someone who "does not know how to obey" will never learn to command.

628 It's gross ineptitude for a Director to be content with a soul rendering four when it could be rendering twelve.

629 You have to obey – and you have to command – always with great love.

630 I would like – help me with your prayer – all of us within Holy Church to feel that we are members of the same body, as the Apostle asks of us. I would like us to be vividly and profoundly aware, without any lack of interest, of the joys, the troubles, the progress of our Mother who is one, holy, catholic, apostolic, Roman.

I would like us to live in unison with one another and all of us with Christ.

631 Convince yourself, my child, that lack of unity within the Church is death.

632 Pray to God that in the Holy Church, our Mother, the hearts of all may be one heart, as they were in the earliest times of Christianity; so that the words of Scripture may be truly fulfilled until the end of the ages: *Multitudinis autem* *credentium erat cor unum et anima una* – the company of the faithful were of one heart and one soul.

–I am saying this to you in all seriousness: may this holy unity not come to any harm through you. Take it to your prayer!

633 Faithfulness to the Pope includes a clear and definite duty: that of knowing his thought, which he tells us in Encyclicals or other documents. We have to do our part to help all Catholics pay attention to the teaching of the Holy Father, and bring their everyday behaviour into line with it.

634 I pray every day with all my heart that God may give us the gift of tongues. Such a gift of tongues does not mean knowing a number of languages, but knowing how to adapt oneself to the capacities of one's hearers.

–It's not a question of "saying foolish things to the crowd so that they understand", but of speaking words of wisdom in clear Christian speech that all can understand.

–This is the gift of tongues that I ask

of Our Lord and of his Holy Mother for all their children.

635 The malice of a few and the ignorance of many – this is the enemy of God and of the Church.

–Let us confound the wicked, and enlighten the minds of the ignorant... With God's help, and with our effort, we will save the world.

636 We have to try to ensure that in all fields of intellectual activity there are upright people, people with a true Christian conscience, who are consistent in their lives, who can use the weapons of knowledge in the service of humanity and of the Church.

Because in the world there will always be, as there were when Jesus came on earth, new Herods who try to make use of scientific knowledge – even if they have to falsify it – to persecute Christ and those who belong to him.

What a great task we have ahead of us!

637 In your work with souls – and all your activity should be work with souls –

be filled with faith, with hope, with love, because all the difficulties will be overcome.

To confirm this truth for us, the Psalmist wrote: *Et tu, Domine, deridebis eos: ad nihilum deduces omnes gentes* – You, O Lord, will laugh at them: You will bring them to nothing.

These words confirm those other words: *Non praevalebunt*; the enemies of God shall not prevail. They will not have any power against the Church, nor against those who serve the Church as instruments of God.

638 Our Holy Mother the Church, in a magnificent extension of love, is scattering the seed of the Gospel throughout the world; from Rome to the outposts of the earth.

–As you help in this work of expansion throughout the whole world, bring those in the outposts to the Pope, so that the earth may be one flock and one Shepherd: one apostolate!

639 *Regnare Christum volumus!*: we want Christ to reign. *Deo omnis gloria!*: all the glory to God.

This ideal of warring, and winning, with Christ's weapons will only become a reality through prayer and sacrifice, through faith and Love.

–Well, then...: pray, believe, suffer, Love!

640 The work of the Church, each day, is a great fabric which we offer to God: because all of us who are baptised are the Church.

–If we carry out our tasks, faithfully and selflessly, this great fabric will be beautiful and flawless. But if someone loosens a thread here, someone else a thread there, and another somewhere else... instead of a beautiful fabric we will have a tattered rag.

641 Why don't you make up your mind to make that fraternal correction? Receiving one hurts, because it is hard to humble oneself, at least to begin with. But making a fraternal correction is always hard. Everyone knows this.

Making fraternal corrections is the best way to help, after prayer and good example.

642 Because of the trust He has placed in you, by bringing you to the Church, you ought to have the balance, the calm, the strength, the human and supernatural prudence of a mature person, that many acquire with the passing of the years.

Don't forget that Christian, as we learnt in the Catechism, means a man or woman who has the faith of Jesus Christ.

643 You want to be strong? Then first realise that you are very weak. After that, trust in Christ, your Father, your Brother, your Teacher. He makes us strong, entrusting to us the means with which to conquer – the sacraments. Live them!

644 I understood you very well when you confessed to me: I want to steep myself in the liturgy of the Holy Mass.

645 How great is the value of piety in the Holy Liturgy!

I was not at all surprised when someone said to me a few days ago, talking about a model priest who had died recently: "What a saint he was!"

–"Did you know him well?" I asked.

–"No," he said, "but I once saw him saying the Mass."

646 Since you call yourself a Christian, you have to live the Sacred Liturgy of the Church, putting genuine care into your prayer and mortification for priests – especially for new priests – on the days marked out for this intention, and when you know that they are to receive the Sacrament of Order.

647 Offer your prayer, your atonement, and your action for this end: *ut sint unum!* – that all of us Christians may share one will, one heart, one spirit. This is so that *omnes cum Petro ad Iesum per Mariam* – that we may all go to Jesus, closely united to the Pope, through Mary.

648 You ask me, my child, what you can do to make me very pleased with you.

–If Our Lord is satisfied with you, then I am too. And you can know that He is happy with you, by the peace and joy in your heart.

649 A clear mark of the man of God, of the woman of God, is the peace in their souls: they have *peace* and they give *peace* to the people they have dealings with.

650 Get used to replying to those poor "haters", when they pelt you with stones, by pelting them with Hail Marys.

651 Don't worry if your work seems barren just now. When it is holiness that is being sown, it is not lost: others will gather in the harvest.

652 Even though you gain little light in your prayer, even though it seems laboured, dry... you should consider, with a sure, ever-new insight, that you need to persevere in every detail of your life of piety.

653 You grew in the face of difficulties in the apostolate when you prayed: "Lord, You are the same as ever. Give me the faith of those men who knew how to correspond to your grace, who worked great miracles, real marvels, in your Name..." And you finished off: "I know that you will do it;

but I also know that you want to be asked. You want to be sought out. You want us to knock hard at the doors of your Heart."

–At the end you renewed your resolve to persevere in humble and trusting prayer.

654 When you are troubled... and also in the hour of success, say again and again, "Lord, don't let go of me, don't leave me, help me as you would a clumsy child; always lead me by the hand!"

655 *Aquae multae non potuerunt exstinguere caritatem!!* – the great turmoil of waters could not quench the fire of charity. –I offer you two interpretations of these words of Holy Scripture. –First: the throng of your past sins, now that you have fully repented of them, will not take you away from the Love of our God; and a second one: the waters of misunderstanding, the difficulties that you are perhaps encountering, should not interrupt your apostolic work.

656 Work on to the end, to the very end! My child, *qui perseveraverit usque in* *finem, hic salvus erit* – it is the one who perseveres right to the end who will be saved.

–We children of God have the means we need: you too! We will finish, we will top out our building, for we can do all things in Him who strengthens us.

–With God there are no *impossibles*. They are overcome always.

657 Sometimes the immediate future is full of worries, if we stop seeing things in a supernatural way.

–So, faith, my child, faith... and more deeds. In that way it is certain that our Father-God will continue to solve your problems.

658 God's ordinary providence is a continual miracle; but He will use extraordinary means when they are required.

659 Christian optimism is not a sugary optimism; nor is it a mere human confidence that everything will turn out all right.

It is an optimism that sinks its roots in an awareness of our freedom, and in the sure knowledge of the power of grace. It is an optimism which leads us to make demands on ourselves, to struggle to respond at every moment to God's calls.

660 The Lord's triumph, on the day of the Resurrection, is final. Where are the soldiers the rulers posted there? Where are the seals that were fixed to the stone of the tomb? Where are those who condemned the Master? Where are those who crucified Jesus?... He is victorious, and faced with his victory those poor wretches have all taken flight.

Be filled with hope: Jesus Christ is always victorious.

661 If you look for Mary, you will *necessarily* find Jesus; and you will learn, in greater and greater depth, what there is in the Heart of God.

662 When you are preparing for a work of apostolate, make your own these words of a man who was seeking God: "Today I start to preach a retreat for priests. God grant we may draw profit from it – and, first of all, myself!"

–And later: "I have been on this retreat for several days now. There are a hundred and twenty on it. I hope that Our Lord will do good work in our souls."

663 My child, it's worth your while being humble, obedient, loyal. Drench yourself in the spirit of God, to carry it from where you are, from your place of work, to all the peoples that fill the earth!

664 During a war, the courage of the soldiers facing the enemy would be of little use if there were not others who seem to take no part in the struggle but who supply the fighting men with armament and food and medicines...

–Without the prayer and sacrifice of many souls there would be no genuine apostolate of action.

665 The power of working miracles! How many dead – and even rotting – souls you will raise, if you let Christ act in you.

In those days, the Gospel tells us, the Lord was passing by; and they, the sick, called to him and sought him out. Now, too, Christ is passing by, in your Christian life. If you second him, many will come to know him, will call to him, will ask him for help: and their eyes will be opened to the marvellous light of grace.

666 You insist on doing your own thing, and so your work is barren.

Obey: be docile. Each cog in a machine must be put in its place. If not, the machine stops, or the parts get damaged. It will surely not produce anything, or if it does, then very little. In the same way, a man or a woman outside his or her proper field of action, will be more of a hindrance than an instrument of apostolate.

667 The apostle has no aim other than letting God work, making himself available.

668 The first Twelve, too, were foreigners in the lands where they taught the Gospel. They came up against people who were building the world on foundations diametrically opposed to Christ's doctrine.

–Look: despite these adverse circumstances, they knew that they had been entrusted with the divine message of the Redemption. And so the Apostle cries, "Woe to me if I do not preach the Gospel!"

669 The co-redeeming – eternal! – efficacy of our lives can only become real with humility, passing unnoticed, so that others can discover Him.

670 The children of God ought to be, with their apostolic action, like those great lighting systems that fill the world with light, but the source is not seen..

671 Jesus says: "He who hears you hears me."

–Do you still think it is your words that convince people?... Don't forget either that the Holy Spirit can carry out his plans with the most useless instrument.

672 Saint Ambrose has some words that fit the children of God marvellously well! He is speaking of the ass's colt, tethered to its dam, which Jesus needed for his triumph: "Only an order of the Lord could untie it", he says. "It was set loose by the hands of the Apostles. To do such a deed, one needs a special way of living and a special grace. You too must be an apostle, to set free those who are captive."

–Let me comment on this text for you once more. How often, upon a word from Jesus, will we have to loosen souls from their bonds, because he needs them for his triumph! May our hands be apostles' hands, and our actions, and our lives also. Then God will give us an apostle's grace, too, to break the fetters of those who are enchained.

673 We can never attribute to ourselves the power of Jesus who is passing by amongst us. Our Lord is passing by: and he transforms souls when we come close to him with one heart, one feeling, one desire: to be good Christians. But it is he who does it: not you nor I. It is Christ who is passing by!

–And then he stays in our hearts – in yours and in mine! – and in our tabernacles.

–Jesus is passing by, and Jesus comes to stay. He stays in you, in each one of you, and in me.

674 Our Lord wants to make us co-redeemers with him.

That is why to help us understand this marvel, he moves the evangelists to tell us of so many great wonders. He could have produced bread from anything... but he doesn't! He looks for human co-operation: he needs a child, a boy, a few pieces of bread and some fish.

He needs you and me: and he is God! This should move us to be generous in our corresponding with his grace.

675 If you help him, even with a trifle, as the Apostles did, He is ready to work miracles; to multiply the bread, to reform wills, to give light to the most benighted minds, to enable those who have never been upright to be so, with an extraordinary grace.

All this he will do... and more, if you will help him with what you have.

676 Jesus has died. He is a corpse. Those holy women had no expectations. They had seen how he had been abused, and how he had been crucified. How vivid in their minds was the violence of the

Passion he had undergone!

They knew, too, that the soldiers were keeping watch over the place. They knew that the tomb was sealed shut: "Who will roll away the stone for us from the door?" they asked themselves, for it was a massive slab. But all the same..., in spite of everything, they went to be with him.

Look: difficulties, large and small, can be seen at once... But if there is love, one pays no heed to those obstacles: one goes ahead with daring, with conviction, with courage. Don't you have to confess your shame when you contemplate the drive, the daring and the courage of these women?

677 Mary, your Mother, will bring you to the Love of Jesus. There you will be *cum gaudio et pace*, with joy and peace. And you will be always "brought", because on your own you would fall and get covered with mud: you will be brought onward, brought to believe, to love, and to suffer.

Work

678 From Saint Paul's teaching, we know that we have to renew the world in the spirit of Jesus Christ, that we have to place Our Lord at the summit and at the heart of all things.

–Do you think you are carrying this out in your work, in your professional task?

679 Why don't you try converting your whole life into the service of God – your work and your rest, your tears and your smiles?

–You can... and you must!

680 Each and every creature, each and every event of this life, without exception, must be steps which take you to God, which move you to know him and love him, to give him thanks, and to strive to make everyone else know and love him.

681 We are under an obligation to work, and to work conscientiously, with a sense of responsibility, with love and perseverance, without any shirking or frivolity. Because work is a command from God, and God is to be obeyed, as the Psalmist says, *in laetitia*, joyfully!

682 We have to conquer for Christ every noble human value.

683 When a person really lives charity, there is no time left for self-seeking. There is no room left for pride. We will not find occasion for anything but service!

684 Every activity – be it of great human importance or not – must become for you a means to serve Our Lord and your fellow men. That is the true measure of its importance.

685 Work always and in everything with sacrifice, to put Christ at the summit of all human activities.

686 Correspondence to grace is to be found also in those very little things of each day, which seem unimportant and yet have the transcendence of Love.

687 You cannot forget that any worthy, noble and honest work at the human level can – and should! – be raised to the supernatural level, becoming a divine task.

688 Jesus, our Lord and Model, growing up and living as one of us, reveals to us that human existence – your life – and its humdrum, ordinary business, have a meaning which is divine, which belongs to eternity.

689 You should be full of wonder at the goodness of our Father God. Are you not filled with joy to know that your home, your family, your country, which you love so much, are the raw material which you must sanctify?

690 My daughter, you have set up a home. I like to remind you that you women – as you well know – have a great strength, which you know how to enfold within a special gentleness, so that it is not noticed. With that strength, you can make your husband and children instruments of God, or demons.

–You will always make them instruments of God: he is counting on your help.

691 I am moved that the Apostle should call Christian marriage *sacramentum magnum* – a great sacrament. From this, too, I deduce the enormous importance of the task of parents.

–You share in the creative power of God: that is why human love is holy, good and noble. It is a gladness of heart which God – in his loving providence – wants others freely to give up.

–Each child that God grants you is a wonderful blessing from him: don't be afraid of children!

692 In conversations I have had with so many married couples, I tell them often that while both they and their children are alive, they should help them to be saints, while being well aware that none of us will be a saint on earth. All we will do is struggle, struggle, struggle.

–And I also tell them: you Christian mothers and fathers are a great spiritual motor, sending the strength of God to your own ones, strength for that struggle, strength to win, strength to be saints. Don't let them down!

693 Don't be afraid of loving others, for His sake: and don't worry about loving your own people even more, provided that no matter how much you love them, you love Him a million times more.

694 *Coepit facere et docere* – Jesus began to do and then to teach. You and I have to bear witness with our example, because we cannot live a double life. We cannot preach what we do not practise. In other words, we have to teach what we are at least struggling to put into practice.

695 Christian: you have the obligation of being an example in all fields: including being an example as a citizen, in your fulfilment of the laws directed to the common good.

696 You are very demanding. You want everyone else, including those who work in the public service, to carry out their obligations. "It is their duty!" you say. Have you then ever thought about whether you respect the timetable of your work and do it conscientiously?

697 Carry out all your duties as a citizen. Do not try to get out of any of your obligations. Exercise all your rights, too, for the good of society, without making any rash exceptions.

–You must give Christian witness in that also.

698 If we really want to sanctify our work, we have inescapably to fulfil the first condition: that of working – and working well! – with human and supernatural seriousness.

699 Your charity should be likeable. Without neglecting prudence or naturalness, try to have, though you may be crying inside, a smile on your lips for everyone at all times, and try to render an unstinting service too.

700 That half-finished work is a caricature of the holocaust, the total offering God is asking of you.

701 If you say that you want to imitate Christ... and yet have time on your hands, then you are going along paths of lukewarmness.

702 Professional work – and working in the home is also a first-class profession – is a witness to the worth of the human creature; a chance to develop one's own personality; a bond of union with others; a fund of resources; a way of helping in the improvement of the society we live in, and of promoting the progress of the whole human race...

–For a Christian, these grand views become even deeper and wider. Because work, which Christ took up as something both redeemed and redeeming, becomes a means, a way of holiness, a specific task which sanctifies and can be sanctified.

703 The Lord wants his children, those of us who have received the gift of faith, to proclaim the original optimistic view of creation, the *love for the world* which is at the heart of Christianity.

–So there should always be enthusiasm in your professional work, and in your effort to build up the earthly city.

704 You must be careful: don't let your professional success or failure – which will certainly come – make you forget, even for a moment, what the true aim of your work is: the glory of God!

705 Christian responsibility in work cannot be limited to just putting in the hours. It means doing the task with technical and professional competence... and, above all, with love of God.

706 What a pity to kill time which is a treasure of God!

707 Since all honest professions can and ought to be sanctified, no child of God has the right to say: I can't do apostolate.

708 From the hidden life of Jesus you must draw this further consequence: not to be in a hurry... even when you are!

That is to say, first and foremost comes the interior life. Everything else, the apostolate, any apostolate, is a corollary.

709 Face up to the problems of this world with a sense of the supernatural, and following the principles of ethics. They do not threaten or undermine your personality: they channel it.

–In this way you will bring to your behaviour a living strength which will win people over; and you will be confirmed in your progress along the right path.

710 God Our Lord wants you to be holy, so that you can make others holy. For this to be possible you need to look at yourself with courage and frankness; you need to look at the Lord Our God; then, and only then, you need to look at the world.

711 Encourage your noble human qualities. They can be the beginning of the building of your sanctification. At the same time, remember what I have already told you before, that when serving God, you have to burn everything, even "what people will say", and even what they call reputation, if necessary.

712 You need formation, because you need a profound sense of responsibility, if you are to foster and encourage the activity of Catholics in public life and do so with the respect that everyone's freedom deserves, reminding each and every one that they have to be consistent with their faith.

713 Through your professional work, which you bring to completion with all the human and supernatural perfection that is possible, you can – and should! – give Christian standards in the places where you carry out your profession or job.

714 As a Christian you have a duty to act and not stand aloof, making your contribution to serve the common good loyally and with personal freedom.

715 We children of God, who are citizens with the same standing as any others, have to take part *fearlessly* in all honest human activities and organizations, so that Christ may be present in them.

Our Lord will ask a strict account of each one of us if through neglect or love of comfort we do not freely strive to play a part in the human developments and decisions on which the present and future of society depend.

716 With a sense of profound humility – strong in the name of our God, and, as the Psalmist says, not "in the numbers of our chariots and of our horses" – we have to make sure, without regard for human considerations, that there are no corners of society where Christ is not known.

717 Freely, according to your own interests and talents, you have to take an active, effective part in the wholesome public or private associations of your country, in a way that is full of the Christian spirit. Such organizations never fail to make some difference to people's temporal or eternal good.

718 Struggle to make sure that those

human institutions and structures in which you work and move with the full rights of a citizen, are in accordance with the principles which govern a Christian view of life.

In this way you can be sure that you are giving people the means to live according to their real worth; and you will enable many souls, with God's grace, to respond personally to their Christian vocation.

719 It is a Christian's duty, and a citizen's duty, to defend and promote, out of piety and general culture, those monuments that are found along streets and highways – the wayside crosses, the statues of Our Lady, and the like. And we should reconstruct those which have been destroyed by vandalism, or the passage of time.

720 We have to stand out boldly against those "damning freedoms" – those daughters of licence, granddaughters of evil passions, great granddaughters of original sin – which come down, as you can see, in a direct line from the devil.

721 For the sake of the objective truth,

and to put a stop to the damage they do, I have to insist that we should give neither publicity nor *hosannas*... to the enemies of God; not even after they are dead.

722 Nowadays our Mother the Church is being attacked in the social field and by the governments of nations. That is why God is sending his children – is sending you! – to struggle, and to spread the truth in those areas.

723 You are an ordinary citizen. It is precisely because of that *secularity* of yours, which is the same as, and neither more nor less than, that of your colleagues, that you have to be sufficiently brave – which may sometimes mean being very brave – to make your faith *felt*. They should see your good works and the motive that drives you to do them.

724 Children of God – like yourself – cannot be afraid of living in the professional or social surroundings which are proper to them. They are never alone!

–God Our Lord, who always goes

with you, grants you the means to be faithful to him, and to bring others to him.

725 All for Love! This is the way of holiness, the way of happiness.

Face up to your intellectual tasks, the highest things of the spirit and also those things that are most down to earth, the things we all of necessity have to do, with this in mind; and you will live joyfully and with peace.

726 As a Christian, you can give way, within the limits of faith and morals, in everything that is your own; you can give way with all your heart... But in what belongs to Jesus Christ, you cannot give way!

727 When you have to give orders, do not humiliate anyone. Go gently. Respect the intelligence and the will of the one who is obeying.

728 Naturally, you have to use earthly means. But put a lot of effort into being detached from everything of the earth, so that you can deal with it with your mind always fixed on the service of God and of your fellow men.

729 Plan everything? Everything! you told me. All right: we need to use our prudence. But bear in mind that human undertakings, whether they are hard or simple, always have to count on a margin of the unforeseen; and that a Christian should never shut off the road of hope, or be forgetful of God's Providence.

730 You have to work with such supernatural vision that you let yourself be absorbed by your activity only in order to make it divine. In this way the earthly becomes divine, the temporal eternal.

731 Things done in the service of God never fail through lack of money: they fail through lack of spirit.

732 Aren't you glad to feel the poverty of Jesus so close to you? How splendid it is to be lacking even what is necessary! But as He did, it must be borne silently and unnoticed.

733 Sincere devotion, true love of God, leads us to work, to fulfil the duty of each day, even though it is far from easy.

734 People have often drawn attention to the danger of deeds performed without any interior life to inspire them; but we should also stress the danger of an interior life – if such a thing is possible – without deeds.

735 The interior struggle doesn't take us away from our temporal business – it makes us finish it off better!

736 Your life cannot be the repetition of actions which are all the same, because the next one should be more upright, more effective, more full of love than the last. Each day should mean new light, new enthusiasm – for Him!

737 Every single day, do what you can to know God better, to *get acquainted* with him, to fall more in love with him each moment, and to think of nothing but of his Love and his glory.

You will carry out this plan, my child, if you never, for any reason whatever, give up your times of prayer, your presence of God, with the aspirations and spiritual communions that set you on fire, your unhurried Holy Mass, and your work, finished off well for him.

738 I will never share the opinion – though I respect it – of those who separate prayer from active life, as if they were incompatible.

We children of God have to be contemplatives: people who, in the midst of the din of the throng, know how to find silence of soul in a lasting conversation with Our Lord, people who know how to look at him as they look at a Father, as they look at a Friend, whom they love madly.

739 Those who are pious, with a piety devoid of affectation, carry out their professional duty perfectly, since they know that their work is a prayer raised to God.

740 Our being children of God, I insist, leads us to have a contemplative spirit in the midst of all human activities; to be light, salt and leaven through our prayer, through our mortification, through our knowledge of religion and of our profession. We will carry out this aim: the more within the world we are, the more we must be God's.

741 Good gold and diamonds lie far down in the depths of the earth, not within everyone's reach.

Your task of holiness – your holiness and that of others – depends on your fervour, your cheerfulness, your everyday, obscure, normal, ordinary work.

742 In our ordinary behaviour we need a power far greater than that of the legendary King Midas, who changed all he touched to gold.

–We have to change, through love, the human work of our usual working day into the work of God: something that will last for ever.

743 If you put your mind to it, everything in your life can be offered to the

Lord, can provide an opportunity to talk with your Father in Heaven, who is always keeping new illumination for you, and granting it to you.

744 Work with cheerfulness, with peace, with presence of God.

–In this way you will also do your task with common sense. You will carry it through to the end. Though tiredness is beating you down, you will finish it off well; and your works will be pleasing to God.

745 You should maintain throughout the day a constant conversation with Our Lord, a conversation fed even by the things that happen in your professional work.

Go in spirit to the Tabernacle... and offer to God the work that is in your hands.

746 From there, where you are working, let your heart escape to the Lord, right close to the Tabernacle, to tell him, without doing anything odd, "My Jesus, I love You".

Don't be afraid to call him so – my

Jesus – and to say it to him often.

747 A priest who was saying the Divine Office prepared himself for prayer in this way: 'I will follow the rule of saying, when I start: "I want to pray as the saints pray", and then I will invite my Guardian Angel to sing the Lord's praises with me.'

Try this in your own vocal prayer, and also as a way of increasing your presence of God in your work.

748 You have received God's call to a specific way: it is to be at all the crossroads of the world, while you remain – doing your professional work – in God.

749 I beg you, don't ever lose the supernatural point of view. Correct your intention as the course of a ship is corrected on the high seas: by looking at the star, by looking at Mary. Then you will always be sure of reaching harbour.

CRUCIBLE

750 I don't ask you to take away my feelings, Lord, because I can use them to serve you with: but I ask you to put them through the crucible.

751 Faced with the marvels of God, and with all our human failures, we have to make this admission: "You are everything to me. Use me as you wish!" Then there will be no more loneliness for you – for us.

752 The great secret of sanctity comes down to becoming more and more like Him, the only and lovable Model.

753 When you pray, but see nothing, and feel flustered and dry, then the way is this: don't think of yourself. Instead, turn your eyes to the Passion of Jesus Christ, our Redeemer.

Be convinced that he is asking each one of us, as he asked those three more intimate Apostles of his in the Garden of Olives, to "Watch and pray."

754 When you open the Holy Gospel, think that what is written there – the words and deeds of Christ – is something that you should not only know, but live. Everything, every point that is told there, has been gathered, detail by detail, for you to make it come alive in the individual circumstances of your life.

–God has called us Catholics to follow him closely. In that holy Writing you will find the Life of Jesus, but you should also find your own life.

You too, like the Apostle, will learn to ask, full of love, "Lord, what would you have me do?..." And in your soul you will hear the conclusive answer, "The Will of God!"

Take up the Gospel every day, then, and read it and live it as a definite rule. This is what the saints have done.

755 If you really want to be sure that your heart is ready to respond, I would recommend you to enter one of the Wounds of Our Lord. In this way you will get to know him closely, you will cleave to him, you will feel his Heart beating... and you will follow him in everything that he asks of you.

756 There can be no doubt that for us who love Jesus, prayer is the great "pain-reliever".

757 The Cross symbolises the life of an apostle of Christ, with a strength and a truth that delight both soul and body, though sometimes it is hard, and we can feel its weight.

758 I understand that, through Love, you want to suffer with Christ – to put your back between him and the executioners who are flogging him, your head instead of his for the thorns, and your hands and feet for the nails. Or at least to accompany our Mother, Holy Mary, on Calvary, and to plead guilty to deicide on account of your sins... and to suffer and to love.

759 You tell me: I have made up my mind to go more often to the Paraclete, to ask him for his light.

–Good. But remember, my child, that the Holy Spirit is a fruit of the Cross.

760 The cheerful love that fills the soul with happiness is founded on suffering. There is no love without renunciation.

761 Christ is nailed to the Cross. And you?... Still taken up with your whims and fancies – or rather, nailed by them!

762 We cannot, must not, be sugar-candy Christians: on earth there must be suffering and the Cross.

763 In this life of ours we must expect the Cross. Those who do not expect the Cross are not Christians, and they will be unable to avoid their own "cross", which will drive them to despair.

764 Now, when the Cross has become a serious and weighty matter, Jesus will see to it that we are filled with peace. He will become our Simon of Cyrene, to lighten the load for us.

Then say to him, trustingly: "Lord, what kind of a Cross is this? A Cross which is no cross. Now I know the trick. It is to abandon myself in you; and from now on, with your help, all my crosses will always be like this."

765 Renew in your own soul the resolution that friend of ours made long ago: "Lord, what I want is suffering, not exhibitionism."

766 To have the Cross is to have found happiness: it is to have you, Lord!

767 What really makes a person – or a whole sector of society – unhappy, is the anxiety-ridden, selfish search for well-being, that desire to get rid of whatever is upsetting.

768 The way of Love is called *Sacrifice.*

769 The Cross, the Holy Cross, is heavy.

–First there are my sins. Then the sad truth of our Mother the Church's suffering;

the apathy of so many Catholics who want without really wanting; the separation – for all kinds of reasons – from those we love; the sufferings and trials of ourselves and of others...

–The Cross, the Holy Cross, is heavy. *Fiat, adimpleatur...!* "May the most just, the most lovable Will of God be done, be fulfilled, be praised and exalted above all things for ever! Amen. Amen."

770 When you walk where Christ walked; when you are no longer just resigned to the Cross, but your whole soul takes on its form – takes on its very shape; when you love the Will of God; when you actually love the Cross... then, only then, is it He who carries it.

771 Join your suffering, your Cross that comes from within or without, to the Will of God, by saying a generous *Fiat!* And you will be filled with joy and with peace.

772 These are the unmistakable signs of the true Cross of Christ: serenity, a deep feeling of peace, a love which is ready for any sacrifice, a great effectiveness which wells from Christ's own wounded Side. And always – and evidently – joy: a joy which comes from knowing that those who truly give themselves are beside the Cross, and therefore beside Our Lord.

773 You must always be aware of and thankful for that favour of the King which throughout your life marks your flesh and your spirit with the royal seal of the Holy Cross.

774 "I carry a little Crucifix", wrote a friend. "Its Crucified is worn out by use and by kisses. It was left to my father when his mother, who had used it, died.

It's a poor thing and much the worse for wear, so I would not have the nerve to give it away to anyone. That's why when I see it my love for the Cross will grow."

775 There was a priest who prayed in a moment of affliction: "Jesus, let whatever Cross You want come to me. I resolve here and now to receive it joyfully, and I bless it with all the richness of my blessing as a priest."

776 When you receive a hard knock, a Cross, you should not be disturbed. Rather the reverse: with a happy face you should give thanks to God.

777 Yesterday I saw a picture which I liked immensely, a picture of Jesus lying dead. An angel was kissing his left hand with an inexpressible devotion. Another, at the Saviour's feet, was holding a nail torn out of the Cross. In the foreground with his back to us there was a tubby little angel weeping as he gazed at Christ.

I prayed to God that they would let me have the picture. It is beautiful. It breathes devotion. I was saddened to hear that they had shown it to a prospective buyer who had refused to take it, saying, "It's a corpse!" To me, You will always be Life.

778 Lord, I have no qualms in repeating this thousands of times: I want to keep you company, suffering with you, in the humiliations and cruelties of your Passion and Cross.

779 To find the Cross is to find Christ.

780 Jesus, may your Divine Blood enter my veins, to make me live the generosity of the Cross at every moment.

781 Look at Jesus hanging dead on the Cross, and pray. In this way the Life and Death of Christ can become the model and the spur of your life, and for your answer to the Will of God.

782 Remember this at the moment of sorrow or expiation: the Cross is the symbol of the redeeming Christ. It has ceased to be the symbol of evil, becoming instead the sign of victory.

783 Among the ingredients of your meal include that *most delicious* one, mortification.

784 It is not the spirit of penance to do great mortifications some days, and nothing on others.

–The spirit of penance means knowing how to overcome yourself every single day, offering up both great and small things for love, without putting on show.

785 If we join our own little things, those insignificant or big difficulties of ours, to the great sufferings of Our Lord, the Victim (He is the only Victim!), their value will increase. They will become a treasure, and then we will take up the Cross of Christ gladly and with style.

–And then every suffering will soon be overcome: nobody, nothing at all, will be able to take away our peace and our joy.

786 To be an apostle you have to bear within you Christ crucified, as Saint Paul teaches us.

787 It's true! When the Holy Cross comes into our lives it unmistakably confirms that we belong to Christ.

788 The Cross is not pain, or annoyance, or bitterness... It is the holy wood on which Jesus Christ triumphs... and where we triumph too, when we receive cheerfully and generously what He sends us.

789 You have come to see that, after the Holy Sacrifice, it is on your Faith and your Love, on your penance, your prayer and your activity, that the perseverance, and even the life on earth of your people to a great extent depend.

–Bless the Cross: the Cross that He – my Lord Jesus – and you and I bear.

790 O Jesus, I want to be a blazing fire of Love-madness. I want it to be sufficient for me just to be present in order to set the world on fire for miles around, with an unquenchable flame. I want to know that I am yours. Then, let the Cross come...

–This is the marvellous way: to suffer, to love, and to believe.

791 When you are ill, offer up your sufferings with love, and they will turn into incense rising up in God's honour, and making you holy.

792 As a child of God, with his grace in you, you have to be a strong person, a man or woman of desires and achievements.

–We are not hothouse plants. We live in the middle of the world, and we have to be able to face up to all the winds that blow, to the heat and the cold, to rain and storms..., but always faithful to God and to his Church.

793 Insults hurt so much, even though you want to love them.

–Don't be surprised: offer them to God.

794 You were very hurt at being slighted! That means you are forgetting too easily who you are.

795 When we think we have been accused of something unjustly, we should examine our behaviour, in God's presence, *cum gaudio et pace* – calmly and cheerfully; and we should change our ways if charity bids us, even if our actions were harmless.

–We have to struggle to be saints, more and more each day. Then let people say what they like so long as we can apply the words of the beatitude to their utterances: *Beati estis cum... dixerint omne malum adversus vos mentientes propter me* – Blessed are you when they slander you for my sake.

796 Someone – I don't remember who, or when – once said that the hurricane of slander always rages against those who are outstanding, just as the wind beats most furiously on the tallest pines.

797 Plots, wretched misinterpretations, cut to the measure of the base hearts that will read them, cowardly insinuations... It is a picture that, sadly, we see over and over again, in different fields. They neither work themselves, nor let others work.

Meditate slowly on those verses of the Psalm: "My God, I have become a stranger to my brothers, an alien to my mother's sons. Because zeal for thy house has consumed me, and the insults of those who insult thee have fallen on me." And keep on working.

798 It is not possible to do good, even among good people, without running into the holy Cross of gossip.

799 *In silentio et in spe erit fortitudo vestra* – in quietness and in trust shall be your strength... This is what the Lord assures to those who are his own. Keep quiet, and trust in him. These are two essential weapons in moments of difficulty, when there doesn't seem to be any human solution.

Look at Jesus in his Holy Passion and Death: suffering borne without complaint is also a measure of love.

800 This is the prayer of a soul who wanted to belong wholly to God, and, for his sake, to all mankind: "Lord, I beg you to work on this sinner, to rectify and purify my intentions, to pass them through the crucible."

801 I was deeply impressed by the willingness to yield of that holy and very learned man, as well as his refusal to give way, when he said "I can come to terms with anything except an offence against God."

802 Think of the good that has been done you throughout your lifetime by those who have injured or attempted to injure you.

–Others call such people their enemies. You should imitate the saints, at least in this. You are nothing so special that you should have enemies; so call them "benefactors". Pray to God for them: as a result, you will come to like them.

803 Listen to me, my child: you must be happy when people treat you badly and dishonour you, when many come out against you excitedly and it becomes the done thing to spit on you, because you are *omnium peripsema*, like the refuse of the world.

–It's hard, it's very hard. It is hard, until at last a man goes to the Tabernacle, seeing himself thought of as the scum of the earth, like a wretched worm, and says with all his heart "Lord, if you don't need my good name, what do I want it for?"

Up to then even that son of God does not know what happiness is – up to that point of nakedness and self-giving, which is a self-giving of love, but founded on mortification, on sorrow.

804 Opposition from good people? It's the devil's doing.

805 When you lose your peace and get nervous, it's like not listening to reason.

At such times, one hears again the

Master's words to Peter as he sank among the waves of his own nerves and lack of peace: "Why did you doubt?"

806 Order will bring harmony to your life, and lead you to perseverance. Order will give peace to your heart, and dignity to your composure.

807 I copy these words for you because they can bring peace to your soul. "My financial situation is as tight as it ever has been. But I don't lose my peace. I'm quite sure that God, my Father, will settle the whole business once and for all.

I want, Lord, to abandon the care of all my affairs into your generous hands. Our Mother – your Mother – will have let you hear those words, now as in Cana: 'They have none!' I believe in you, I hope in you, I love you, Jesus. I want nothing for myself: it's for them."

808 I love your Will. I love holy poverty, my own great lady.

–And, now and for ever, I detest and abominate anything that might mean the slightest lack of attachment to your most just, most lovable, and most fatherly Will.

809 The spirit of poverty, of detachment from the goods of the earth, results in effectiveness in the apostolate.

810 Nazareth: a way of faith, of detachment: a way in which the Creator subjects himself to his creatures as he does to his Heavenly Father.

811 Jesus always speaks with love... even when he corrects us or allows us to undergo trials.

812 Identify yourself with the Will of God. Then no trouble will be any trouble.

813 God loves us infinitely more than you love yourself... So let him make demands on you!

814 Accept God's Will fearlessly. Resolve unhesitatingly to work all your life, with the materials which the teachings and the demands of our Faith provide.

–If you do, you can be sure that along with the sufferings, and even along with slander, you will be happy, with a happiness that will move you to love others and give them a share in your supernatural joy.

815 If troubles come, you can be sure they are a proof of the Fatherly love God has for you.

816 In the forge of suffering that accompanies the life of all who love, the Lord teaches us that those who tread fearlessly where the Master treads, hard though the going is, find joy.

817 Strengthen your spirit with penance, so that when difficulty comes you may never lose heart.

818 When will you make up your mind, once and for all, to identify yourself with Christ, with Life!

819 To persevere in following in the footsteps of Jesus, you always need a continuous freedom, a continuous willingness, a continuous exercise of your own freedom.

820 You are amazed to find that in each of the possibilities for improvement there are many different goals...

–They are other ways within *the way*, and they help you to avoid possible routine and bring you closer to Our Lord.

–Be generous: aim for the highest.

821 Work with humility. I mean, count first on God's blessings, which will not fail you. Then, on your good desires, on your work plans – and on your difficulties! Do not forget that among those difficulties you must always include your own lack of holiness.

–You will be a good instrument if every day you struggle to be better.

822 You told me, in confidence, that in your prayer you would open your heart to God with these words: "I think of my wretchedness, which seems to be on the increase in spite of the graces you give me. It must be due to my failure to correspond.

I know that I am completely unprepared for the enterprise you are asking of me. And when I read in the newspapers of so very many highly qualified and respected men, with talents and money, speaking, writing, organizing in defence of your reign... I look at myself, and see that I'm a nobody: ignorant, poor: so little, in a word. This would fill me with shame if I did not know that you want me to be so. But Lord Jesus, you know how very gladly I have put my ambition at your feet... To have Faith and Love, to be loving, believing, suffering. In these things I *do* want to be rich and learned: but no more rich or learned than you, in your limitless Mercy, have wanted me to be. I desire to put all my prestige and honour into fulfilling your most just and most lovable Will."

–I then said to you: don't let this remain merely as a good desire.

823 Love for God invites us to shoulder the Cross squarely: to feel on our back the weight of the whole human race, and to fulfil, in the circumstances of our own situation in life and the job we have, the clear and at the same time loving designs of the Will of the Father.

824 He was the greatest madman of all times. What greater madness could there be than to give oneself as he did, and for such people?

It would have been mad enough to have chosen to become a helpless Child. But even then, many wicked men might have been softened, and would not have dared to harm him. So this was not enough for him. He wanted to make himself even less, to give himself more lavishly. He made himself food, he became Bread.

–Divine Madman! How do men treat you? How do I treat you?

825 Jesus, the madness of your Love has stolen my heart. You are small and helpless, so that those who eat you can become great.

826 You have to make your life essentially, totally eucharistic.

827 I like to call the Tabernacle a prison

– a prison of Love.

–For twenty centuries He has been waiting there, willingly locked up, for me and for everyone.

828 Have you ever thought how you would prepare yourself to receive Our Lord if you could go to Communion only once in your life?

–We must be thankful to God that he makes it so easy for us to come to him: but we should show our gratitude by preparing ourselves very well to receive him.

829 Tell Our Lord that from now on, every time you celebrate Mass or attend it, and every time you administer or receive the Sacrament of the Eucharist, you will do so with a great faith, with a burning love, just as if it were to be the last time in your life.

–And be sorry for the carelessness of your past life.

830 I can understand your keenness to receive the Holy Eucharist each day, because those who feel they are children of God have an overpowering need of Christ.

831 While you are at Mass, think that you are sharing in a divine Sacrifice. For that is how it is: on the altar, Christ is offering himself again for you.

832 When you receive him, tell him: Lord, I hope in you: I adore you, I love you, increase my faith. Be the support of my weakness: You, who have remained defenceless in the Eucharist so as to be the remedy for the weakness of your creatures.

833 By a process of assimilation we should make these words of Jesus our own: *Desiderio desideravi hoc Pascha manducare vobiscum*: I have longed and longed to eat this Passover with you. There is no better way to show how great is our concern and love for the Holy Sacrifice than by taking great care with the least detail of the ceremonies the wisdom of the Church has laid down.

This is for Love: but we should also feel the *need* to become like Christ, not only inside ourselves but also in what is external. We should act, on the wide spaciousness of the Christian altar, with the rhythm and harmony which obedient holiness provides, uniting us to the will of the Spouse of Christ, to the Will of Christ himself.

834 We should receive Our Lord in the Eucharist as we would prepare to receive the great ones of the earth, or even better: with decorations, with lights, with new clothes...

–And if you ask me what sort of cleanliness I mean, what decorations and what lights you should bring, I will answer you: cleanliness in each one of your senses, decoration in each of your powers, light in all your soul.

835 Be a eucharistic soul!

–If the centre around which your thoughts and hopes turn is the Tabernacle, then, my child, how abundant the fruits of your sanctity and apostolate will be!

836 The objects used in divine worship should have artistic merit, but bearing in mind that worship is not for the sake of art: art is for the sake of worship.

837 Go perseveringly to the Tabernacle, either bodily or in your heart, so as to feel safe and calm: but also to feel loved... and to love!

838 I copy some words which a priest wrote for those who followed him in an apostolic enterprise: "When you contemplate the Sacred Host exposed on the altar in the monstrance, think how great is the love, the tenderness of Christ. My way to understand it is by thinking of the love I have for you: if I could be far away, working, and at the same time at the side of each one of you, how gladly I would do it!

But Christ really can do it! He loves us with a love that is infinitely greater than the love that all the hearts of the world could hold; and he has stayed with us so that we can join ourselves at any time to his most Sacred Humanity, and so that he can help us, console us, strengthen us, so that we may be faithful."

839 Don't think that turning your life into service is easy. This good desire needs to be translated into deeds, for "the kingdom of God does not consist in talk, but in power", as the Apostle teaches us. Moreover, the practice of constantly helping other people is not possible without sacrifice.

840 You must always have, in everything, the same "sentiments" as the Church. For this, you must acquire the spiritual and doctrinal training that you need, which will make you a person of sound judgement in temporal matters, humble and quick to correct yourself when you realise you have made a mistake.

–Correcting your own mistakes, nobly, is a very human and very supernatural way of using your freedom.

841 There is an urgent need for spreading the doctrine of Christ.

Store up your training, fill yourself with clear ideas, with the fullness of the Christian message, so that afterwards you can pass it on to others.

–Don't expect God to illuminate you, for he has no reason to when you have definite human means available to you: study and work.

842 Error does not only darken the understanding: it also sunders wills.

But *veritas liberabit vos*: the truth will set you free from the partisan spirit that dries up charity.

843 You spend your time with that companion of yours who is scarcely even civil to you... and it's hard.

–Keep at it, and don't judge him. He'll have his "reasons", just as you have yours, which you strengthen so as to pray for him more each day.

844 If you walk in the world on all fours, how can you be surprised if other people are not angels?

845 Be lovingly on your guard, to live holy purity, because a spark is more easily put out than a roaring blaze.

But all human care, and mortification, and the cilice, and fasting – which are essential weapons! – how little all these are worth without you, my God!

846 Constantly call to mind that at

every moment you are cooperating in the human and spiritual formation of those around you, and of all souls – for the blessed Communion of Saints reaches as far as that. At every moment: when you work and when you rest; when people see you happy or when they see you worried; when at your job, or out in the middle of the street, you pray as does a child of God and the peace of your soul shows through; when people see that you have suffered, that you have wept, and you smile.

847 Holy coercion is one thing; blind violence or revenge is quite another.

848 The Master has said it already: if only we children of the light were to put at least as much effort and *obstinacy* into doing good as the children of darkness put into their activities!

–Don't complain. Work, instead, to drown evil in an abundance of good!

849 The charity that harms the supernatural effectiveness of the apostolate is a false charity.

850 God needs women and men who are sure and strong, on whom he can lean.

851 We do not live for the world, or for our own honour, but for the honour of God, for the glory of God, for the service of God. It is this that should be our motive!

852 Ever since Jesus Christ Our Lord founded the Church, this Mother of ours has suffered continual persecution. Perhaps in other times persecution was carried out openly, while nowadays it is often done surreptitiously: but today as yesterday the Church continues to be attacked.

–How great is our obligation to live every day as responsible Catholics!

853 Use this prescription for your life: "I don't remember that I exist. I don't think of my own affairs, because there is no time left."

–Work and service!

854 These are the characteristics that define the incomparable goodness of our holy Mother, Mary: a love taken to the extreme, fulfilling the Will of God with tender care; a complete forgetfulness of herself, for she is happy to be where God wants her to be.

–For this reason, not even the slightest gesture of hers is trivial. Learn from her.

SELECTION

855 Committed! How much I like that word! We children of God freely put ourselves under an obligation to live a life of dedication to God, striving that He may have complete and absolute sovereignty over our lives.

856 Whenever sanctity is genuine, it overflows from its vessel to fill other hearts, other souls, with its superabundance.

We, the children of God, sanctify ourselves by sanctifying others. Is Christian life growing around you? Consider this every day.

857 The Kingdom of Jesus Christ: that is our task! So, my child, be generous:

don't be anxious to know any of the many reasons he has to want to reign in you.

If you look at him, it will be enough for you to consider how much he loves you... You will feel a hunger to correspond to his love, crying aloud that you really love him here and now; and you will understand that if you don't leave him, he won't leave you.

858 The first step towards bringing others to the ways of Christ is for them to see you happy and serene, sure in your advance towards God.

859 A Catholic man or woman can never forget this key idea: we have to imitate Jesus Christ in every sphere of society, without rejecting anyone.

860 Our Lord Jesus wants it: we have to follow him closely. There is no other way.

This is the task of the Holy Spirit in each soul, in yours too. You have to be docile, so as not to put obstacles in the way of your God.

861 A clear sign that you are seeking holiness is – allow me to use the expression – 'the healthy psychological prejudice' of thinking habitually about others, while forgetting yourself, so as to bring them closer to God.

862 It should be engraved deeply on your soul that God doesn't need you. His calling is a most loving mercy of his Heart.

863 Treat those who are in error with loving kindness, with Christian charity. But do not compromise with anything that goes against our holy Faith.

864 Have recourse to the sweet Lady Mary, Mother of God and our Mother also, entrusting to her care the cleanliness of soul and body of all mankind.

Tell her that you want to call upon her, and want others to call upon her continually. And that you want to conquer always, in the bad moments – or the good, and very good moments – of your struggle against those who are hostile to our being children of God.

865 He came on earth because *omnes homines vult salvos fieri*, he wants to redeem the whole world.

–While you are at your work, shoulder to shoulder with so many others, never forget that there is no soul that does not matter to Christ!

866 "Lord!," you were telling him, "I like to say thank you. I want to be grateful to everyone, always."

–Well, look: you aren't a stone... or a speechless tree... or a mule. You are not one of those created things whose life is completed here on this earth. This is because God chose to make you a man or woman, a child of his. And he loves you *in caritate perpetua*, with an eternal love.

–So you like to be grateful? And are you going to make an exception of your Lord? Make sure that your thanksgiving comes pouring out from your heart every day.

867 Understanding is real charity. When you really achieve it, you will have a great heart which is open to all without discrimination. Even with those who have treated you badly you will put into living practice that advice of Jesus: "Come to me all you that... are heavy laden, and I will give you rest."

868 Be loving towards those who are ignorant of the things of God. And with all the more reason treat in that same way those who know him. If not, you cannot do the former either.

869 If you really loved God with all your heart, then that love for your neighbour, which you sometimes find so hard to have, would come as a necessary consequence of your Great Love. You would never feel hostility towards anyone, nor would you discriminate between people.

870 Have you that urge, that divine madness, to bring souls to know the Love of God? In your ordinary life, then, offer up mortifications, pray, do your duty, and conquer yourself in all kinds of tiny details.

871 Tell him slowly: Good Jesus, if I am to be an apostle, and an apostle of apostles, you have to make me very humble.

May I know myself. May I know myself and know you.

–Then I will never lose sight of my nothingness.

872 *Per Jesum Christum Dominum nostrum*: through Jesus Christ, Our Lord. That is the way you should do things: through and for Jesus Christ!

–It's good that you have a human heart. But if you act merely because it's a particular person, that's bad. You should certainly also do it for that brother of yours, for that friend of yours: but above all do it for Jesus Christ!

873 The Church, the souls, of all continents, of all times present and to come, expect a lot from you... But you should have it very firmly fixed in your head and in your heart that you will be fruitless if you are not a saint or, let me put it better, if you don't struggle to be a saint.

874 Let yourself be formed by the rough or gentle strokes of grace. Strive to be an instrument rather than an obstacle. And, if you are willing, your most Holy Mother will help you; and you will be a channel for the waters of God, rather than a boulder which diverts their flow.

875 Lord, help me to be faithful and docile towards you, *sicut lutum in manu figuli*, like clay in the potter's hands. In this way it will not be I that live, but you, my Love, who will live and work in me.

876 Jesus will enable you to have a great affection for everybody you meet, without taking away any of the affection you have for him. On the contrary, the more you love Jesus, the more room there will be for other people in your heart.

877 The closer a creature comes to God, the more universal it feels. Its heart expands, making room for everything and everybody in its single great desire to place the whole universe at the feet of Jesus.

878 When Jesus died on the Cross he was only thirty-three years old. Youthfulness can be no excuse!

Anyway, with each day that passes you are ceasing to be young... though with Him you will possess his eternal youth.

879 You must reject that form of nationalism which hinders understanding and harmony. In many moments of history it has been one of the most evil of barriers.

You must reject it yet more strongly, since it would be all the more harmful, when it tries to set foot within the Body of the Church, where the unity of everyone and everything in the love of Jesus Christ ought to shine out most clearly.

880 Child of God, what have you done up to now to help the souls around you?

–You cannot be content with that passiveness, with that idleness of yours. He wants to reach others through your example, through your words, through your friendship, through your service...

881 Sacrifice yourself, give yourself, and work at souls one by one, as the jeweller works on precious stones: one by one.

–Indeed you should exercise even more care, because you are dealing with something of incomparable value. The purpose of that spiritual attention you give is to prepare good instruments for the service of God: and they, each one of them, have cost Christ all of his Blood.

882 To be a Christian, and in particular to be a priest –bearing in mind, too, that all of us who are baptized share in Christ's priesthood – is to be at all times on the Cross.

883 If you were consistent, now that you have seen his light you would want to be as great a saint as you were once a sinner: and you would struggle to make those desires a reality.

884 It is not pride, but fortitude, when you make your authority felt, cutting out what needs to be cut out, when the fulfilment of the Holy Will of God demands it.

885 Hands must sometimes be tied, with respect and with temperateness, without insult or discourtesy. Not out of revenge, but as a remedy; not as a punishment, but as a medicine.

886 You looked at me very seriously... But at last you understood, when I told you: "I want to reproduce the life of Christ in the children of God, by getting them to meditate on it, so that they may act like him and speak only of him."

887 Jesus has remained within the Eucharist for love... of you.

–He remained, knowing how men would receive him... and how you would receive him.

–He has remained so that you could eat him, so that you could visit him and tell him about your things; and so that you could talk to him as you pray beside the Tabernacle, and as you receive the Sacrament; and so that you could fall in love more and more each day, and make other souls, *many souls*, follow the same path.

888 You tell me that you want to practise holy poverty, you want to be detached from the things you use. Ask yourself this question: do I have the same affections and the same feelings as Jesus Christ has, with regard to riches and poverty?

I told you: as well as resting in the arms of your Father-God, with all the confident abandonment of one who is his child, you should fix your eyes particularly on this virtue to love it as Jesus does. Then, instead of seeing it as a cross to bear, you will see it as a sign of God's special love for you.

889 At times, in their behaviour, some Christians don't give the commandment of charity the full scope and value it has. In that last wonderful discourse of his, we find Christ surrounded by his chosen ones and leaving them these words as a form of testament: *Mandatum novum do vobis, ut diligatis invicem* – a new commandment I give to you, that you love one another.

Then he went further: *In hoc cognoscent omnes quia discipuli mei estis* – by this all men will know that you are my disciples, if you have love for one another.

–If only we would make up our minds to live as he wants!

890 If piety is lacking – the bond which ties us close to God and, for his sake, to others because we see Christ in them – disunity is inevitable, with the loss of all Christian spirit.

891 Be grateful to God from the bottom of your heart for those wonderful and awesome faculties he chose to give you when he made you – your intellect and your will. They are wonderful, because they make you like him; and awesome because there are human beings who turn their faculties against their Creator.

It seems to me we could sum up the thankfulness that we owe as children of God by saying to this Father of ours, now and always, *serviam!*: I will serve you!

892 Without interior life, and without formation, there is no true apostolate and no work that is fruitful. Whatever work is done will be fragile, fictitious even.

–How great, then, is our responsibility as children of God! We have to hunger and thirst for him and for his doctrine.

893 Someone told that good friend of ours, seeking to humiliate him, that his was a second- or third-rate soul.

As he was convinced of his nothingness, he was not upset. Instead he reasoned this way: "Each man has just one soul. I have mine, just the one. So for each one his own soul is first-rate. I'm not going to lower my sights. So, my soul is of the very very best: and with God's help, I want to purify it and whiten it and set it on fire, to please my Beloved."

–You must not forget this: you cannot "lower your sights" either, despite the fact that you see yourself full of wretchedness.

894 You complain that you are alone, and that your surroundings militate against you. Think of this, then: Jesus, the Good Sower, takes each of us, his children, and holds us tight in his wounded hand, like wheat. He soaks us in his Blood. He purifies and cleanses us. He fills us with his "wine"! And then he scatters us generously throughout the world, one by one, for wheat is not sown by the sackful, but grain by grain.

895 I insist: ask God to grant us, his children, the "gift of tongues", the gift of making ourselves understood by all.

You can find the reason why I want this "gift of tongues" in the pages of the Gospel, which abound in parables, in examples which materialise the doctrine and illustrate spiritual truths, without debasing or degrading the word of God.

Everyone, both the learned and the less learned, finds it easier to reflect on and understand God's message through these human images.

896 At this time – and always! – when the Lord wants his seed to spread in a divine diffusion among the different surroundings, he also wants the extension not to lessen in intensity.

And you have the clear and supernatural mission of helping to ensure that this intensity is not lost.

897 Yes, you're right: the depth of your wretchedness! By your own efforts, where would you be now, where would you have got to?

You admitted: "Only a Love that was full of mercy could keep on loving me."

–Cheer up. He will not deny you his Love or his Mercy, if you seek him.

898 Your aim should be that there be many souls in the midst of the world who love God with all their heart.

–It's time to do your sums: how many souls have you helped to discover that Love?

899 The children of God are present and give witness in the world to draw others, not to be drawn by them. They should spread their own atmosphere, the atmosphere of Christ, not let themselves be won over by a different atmosphere.

900 You have a duty to reach those around you, to shake them out of their drowsiness, to open wide new horizons for their selfish, comfortable lives, to "complicate" their lives in a holy way, to make them forget about themselves and show understanding for the problems of others.

If you do not, you are not a good brother to your brothers in the human race, who need that *gaudium cum pace*, that joy and that peace, which maybe they do not know or have forgotten.

901 No son or daughter of Holy Church can lead a quiet life, without concern for the anonymous masses – a mob, a herd, a flock, as I once wrote. How many noble passions they have within their apparent listlessness! How much potential!

We must serve all, laying our hands on each and every one, as Jesus did, *singulis manus imponens*, to bring them back to life, to enlighten their minds and strengthen their wills: so that they can become useful!

902 I didn't think God would get hold of me the way he did, either. But, let me tell you once again, God doesn't ask our permission to "complicate" our lives. He just gets in: and that's that!

903 Lord, I will trust in you alone. Help me to be faithful to you. I know that I can look forward to everything as a result of being faithful in your service, abandoning all my cares and worries in your hands.

904 Let us thank God deeply and often for the wonderful calling we have had from him. May our gratitude be deep and genuine, closely joined to humility.

905 The privilege of being numbered among the children of God is the greatest happiness; it is always undeserved.

906 That cry of the Son of God, lamenting that the harvest is plentiful but the labourers are few, is always relevant. How it tears at our heartstrings.

–That cry came from Christ's mouth for you to hear too. How have you responded to it up to now? Do you pray at least daily for that intention ?

907 To follow Our Lord you need to give yourself once and for all, stout-heartedly and without holding anything back – to burn your boats once and for all, so that there is no chance of going back.

908 Don't be scared when Jesus asks you for more, even the happiness of your own family. You must be convinced that from the supernatural point of view he has the right to override all your people, for the sake of his Glory.

909 You say that you want to be an apostle of Christ.

–I'm very glad to hear it. I pray that God may give you perseverance. Remember that from our mouths, from our thoughts, from our hearts, should issue only divine motives, of hunger for souls, of themes that lead us one way or another to God – or at least, that do not take you away from him.

910 The Church needs priests, and always will. Ask the Blessed Trinity for them each day, through Holy Mary.

–And pray that they may be cheerful, hard-working, effective; that they may be well trained: and that they may sacrifice themselves joyfully for their brothers, without feeling that they are victims.

911 Turn constantly to the most Holy

Virgin, the Mother of God and Mother of the human race; and she, with a Mother's gentleness, will draw down the love of God on the souls you deal with, so that they may make up their minds to be witnesses for Jesus Christ, in their profession, in their ordinary work.

Fruitfulness

912 You should correspond to God's love by being faithful, very faithful! And this faithfulness should lead you to transmit the Love you have received to other people, so that they too may rejoice at meeting God.

913 My Lord Jesus, grant that I may feel your grace and second it in such a way that I empty my heart... so that you may fill it, my Friend, my Brother, my King, my God, my Love!

914 If your prayers, your sacrifices and your actions do not show a constant concern for the apostolate, it is a sure sign that you are not happy, and that you have to be more faithful.

–Whoever possesses happiness, and the good, will always seek to give it to others.

915 When you really trample on your own self and live for others, then you will become a good instrument in God's hands.

He called – and is calling – his disciples, commanding them *ut eatis!* – "Go and seek all men."

916 Make up your mind to set the world ablaze – you can – in loves that are pure, to make all mankind happy by bringing them really closer to God.

917 *In modico fidelis!* – faithful in little things. Your job, my son, is not just to save souls but to bring them to holiness, day after day, giving to each moment – even to apparently commonplace moments – the dynamic echo of eternity.

918 We cannot separate the seed of doctrine from the seed of piety.

The only way to inoculate your work of sowing doctrine against the germs of ineffectiveness is by being sincerely devout.

919 Just as all the powerful machinery in dozens of factories is brought to a standstill and rendered useless when the electricity fails, so does apostolate cease to bear fruit when prayer and mortification fail, for they are what move the Sacred Heart of Christ.

920 If you follow faithfully the promptings of grace, you will yield good fruit, lasting fruit for the glory of God.

–To be a saint necessarily entails being effective, even though the saint may not see or be aware of the results.

921 Rectitude of intention consists in seeking "only and in all things" the glory of God.

922 The apostolate – which is a sure sign of spiritual life –means being constantly on the lookout so as to supernaturalise each detail of the day, whether big or small, by putting the love of God into everything one does.

923 As a bookmark for whatever book

he happened to be reading, he always used a strip of paper with this motto written on it in a bold and energetic hand: *Ure igne Sancti Spiritus!* –You could almost say that, rather than writing the words, he had engraved them: Inflame with the fire of the Holy Spirit!

O Christian, engraved on your soul and burning on your lips and caught fast in your works, I would like to leave that divine fire.

924 You should try to have the holy shamelessness of a child who *knows* that his Father God always sends him what is best.

That is why even when the apparently most necessary things are lacking he doesn't worry; and with complete serenity he says: I still have the Holy Spirit and he remains with me.

925 Please say a prayer each day for the following intention: that all of us Catholics may be faithful and determined to struggle to be saints.

–It is so obviously reasonable. What else are we to desire for those we love, for those who are bound to us by the strong ties of the faith?

926 When I am told that there are people dedicated to God who are no longer striving with fervour for sanctity, I think that – if there is any truth in this – their lives are heading towards great failure.

927 *Qui sunt isti, qui ut nubes volant, et quasi columbae ad fenestras suas?* – "Who are these that fly like clouds, and like doves to their nesting places?", asks the Prophet. And a certain author comments: "Clouds come up from the sea and from rivers, and after circling about or following their course for a certain length of time, return once more to their source."

And I say to you that this is what you have to be: a cloud which makes the world fertile, making it live the life of Christ. Those divine waters will bathe and drench the very depths of the earth, and filter out the many impurities without themselves being dirtied. Sparkling springs will flow from them that will later become streams and mighty rivers able to slake the thirst of mankind. Afterwards you shall return to your Shelter, to your boundless Sea, to your God, knowing that the fruits will continue to ripen thanks to the supernatural watering done by your apostolate, and to the fruitfulness of the waters of God which will last until the end of time.

928 My child, offer him even the sorrows and sufferings of other people.

929 Woes? Setbacks deriving from one thing or another? Can't you see that this is the will of your Father-God... He is good... and He loves you – loves *you* personally – more than all the mothers in the world can possibly love their children?

930 Sincerely examine the way you are following the Master. Consider whether you might have given yourself in a dry, official way, with a faith that has no sparkle to it; if there is no humility or sacrifice, nor daily work; if you are all façade and pay no attention to the details of each moment... In a word, if you lack Love.

If this is the case, your ineffectiveness should come as no surprise to you. React right away, and be led by the hand of Our Lady.

931 Whenever you are in need of anything, or are facing difficulties, whether great or small, invoke your Guardian Angel, asking him to sort the matter out with Jesus, or to do the particular service you may require.

932 God is right there in the centre of your soul, and mine, and in the soul of everyone who is in a state of grace. He is there for a purpose: so that our salt may increase, that we may acquire more light and that each one of us from his place may know how to distribute those gifts of God.

And how can we share out these gifts from God? With humility and piety, and by being very united to our Mother the Church.

–Do you not recall the vine and the branches? How fruitful is each branch when united to the vine! What large bunches of grapes! And how sterile the broken-off branch that dries up and becomes lifeless!

933 Jesus, may my poor heart be filled

from the ocean of your Love, with such big waves that can cleanse me and expel from me all my wretchedness. Pour those most pure and ardent waters of your Heart into mine, until my desires for loving you are fully satisfied and I can no longer hold back my response to your divine ardour. My heart shall surely break then, dying for Love, and pour out that Love of yours which, in irresistible and most fertile, life-giving torrents, will reach other hearts that will beat through contact with these living waters, with the pulsating force of Faith and Charity.

934 Live the Holy Mass!

–You may be helped by a consideration which that priest, in love, used to repeat to himself: “Is it possible, my God, to take part in the Holy Mass and not be a saint?”

–And he would continue, “Each day, in fulfilment of an old promise, I will remain hidden in the Wound of Our Lord’s Side!”

–Shouldn’t you do the same?

935 You can do so much good, and so much harm!

–You will do good if you are humble

and you give yourself cheerfully, with a spirit of sacrifice: good for yourself and for your fellow men, and for that good Mother, the Church.

–And how much harm if you allow yourself to be led by your pride.

936 Please don't let yourself become *bourgeois*, for if you do, you will be a hindrance. You will become a dead weight for others in the apostolate and, above all, a source of suffering for the Heart of Christ.

You must not stop doing apostolate, nor abandon your effort to do your work as best you can, nor neglect your life of piety.

–God will do the rest.

937 From time to time you have to deal with souls as you would with a fire in the hearth, giving it a good poke to get rid of the embers, which are what shine most but are causing the fire of the love of God to die down.

938 Let us go to Jesus in the Tabernacle where we can get to know him and assimilate his teaching, and then be able to hand out this food to souls.

939 When you hold Our Lord in your breast and you taste the delights of his Love, promise him that you will strive to change the course of your life in whatever way is necessary, so that you can bring him to the masses of people who do not know him, who live without ideals and who, unfortunately, go on behaving like animals.

940 "Where charity and love are found, there is God" we sing in the liturgical hymn. Here is what a certain soul noted down: "Fraternal love is a great and marvellous treasure. It is not simply a consolation – which it certainly often has to be – but it really brings home the certainty of having God close to us, and shows itself in the charity our neighbours have for us and in the charity which we have for them."

941 Shun public display! May your life be known to God, for holiness passes unnoticed, even though it is most effective.

942 Try to ensure that people don't

notice when you lend a helping hand; try not to be praised or seen by anyone... so that, being hidden like salt, you may give flavour to your normal surroundings. And thus, as a result of your Christian outlook, you will be helping to give to everything about you a natural, loving and attractive tone.

943 For this world of ours to set its course in a Christian direction – which is the only one worthwhile – we have to exercise a loyal friendship with all men, based on a prior loyal friendship with God.

944 You have heard me speak many times about the apostolate *ad fidem*.

I still think the same way. What a marvellous field of work awaits us throughout the world with those who do not know the true faith and who, nonetheless, are noble, generous and cheerful.

945 I often feel like shouting in the ears of so many men and women in offices and shops, in the world of the media and in the law courts, in schools, on the factory floor, in mines and on farms and telling them that, with the backing of an interior life and by means of the Communion of Saints, they ought to be bringing God into all these different environments, according to that teaching of the Apostle: "Glorify God with your life and carry him always with you. by making your bodies the shrines of his presence."

946 Those of us who bear in our hearts the truth of Christ have to put this truth into the hearts, and minds and lives of others. Not to do so would show a love of comfort and bad tactics too.

Think it over once again: Did Christ ask you permission before coming into your soul? He left you free to follow him, but he was the one who sought you out, because he chose to.

947 With our acts of service we can prepare an even greater triumph for the Lord than that of his entry into Jerusalem. For there will be no repetition of the Judas episode, or that of the Garden of Gethsemane, or of that dark night. We will succeed in setting the world alight with the flames of that fire which he came to cast upon the earth! And the light of Truth – which is our Jesus – will enlighten men's minds in an unending day.

948 I beg you, don't be so shocked! As a Christian you have the right and the duty to provoke a wholesome crisis in souls so that they live their lives with their eyes on God.

949 Pray for everyone, for people of every race and tongue and of every creed, for those who have only a vague idea about religion and for those who do not know the faith.

–And this zeal for souls, which is a sure and a clear sign that we love Jesus, will make Jesus come.

950 When they heard of work with souls in far-off lands, how their eyes sparkled! They seemed ready to cross the ocean in one leap. And indeed the world is very small when Love is great.

951 Not a single soul – not one! – can be a matter of indifference to you.

952 A disciple of Christ can never think as follows: "I try to be good; as for others, if that's what they want... let them go to hell."

Such an attitude is not human. Nor is it in keeping with the love of God, or with the charity we owe our neighbour.

953 When a Christian understands what catholicity means and practises it, and he realises the urgent need to proclaim the Good News of salvation to all creatures, he knows that as the Apostle teaches, he has to make himself "all things to all men, that all may be saved."

954 You have to love your fellow men to the point where even their defects, as long as they do not constitute an offence against God, hardly seem to you to be defects at all. If you love only the good qualities you see in others – if you do not know how to be understanding, to make allowances for them and forgive them – you are an egoist.

955 You must not destroy the souls of your fellow human beings through your neglect or your bad example.

–In spite of your passions, you have a responsibility for the Christian life of your neighbour, for the spiritual effectiveness of everyone, indeed for their very sanctity.

956 Physically far away and yet feeling very close to them all, "very close to them all..." you cheerfully repeated.

You were happy thanks to that communion of charity which I spoke to you about, and which you must not get tired of keeping alive.

957 You asked me what you could do to prevent the loneliness of that friend of yours.

–I will tell you what I always say, because we have at our disposal a marvellous weapon which is the answer to everything: prayer. In the first place, you must pray. And then you must do for him what you would like others to do for you if you were in similar circumstances.

Without humiliating him, you must help him in such a way that what he finds difficult is made easy.

958 Put yourself always in your neighbour's shoes. You will then see the various issues or problems calmly. You will not get annoyed. You will be understanding. You will make allowances and will correct people when and as required. And you will fill the world with charity.

959 We cannot give way in matters of faith. But don't forget that in order to speak the truth there is no need to ill-treat anyone.

960 When the good of your neighbour is at stake you cannot remain silent. But speak in a kindly way, with due moderation and without losing your temper.

961 It's not possible to comment on events or doctrines without making personal references..., although you are not judging anyone: *qui judicat Dominus est* – it is God who has to judge.

–Don't worry, then, if now and again you come across someone who lacks an upright conscience and – either in bad faith or through lack of discernment – takes your words for gossip.

962 Some poor people seem to get annoyed by the good works you are doing, as if a thing ceases to be good when it is not being carried out or organized by themselves.

–This lack of understanding cannot be an excuse for you to slacken off in what you are doing. Try to do it even better, right now. When you get no applause on earth, your work will be all the more welcome in Heaven.

963 At times, fifty per cent of the work is lost because of in-fighting stemming from a lack of charity, and from tales and back-biting among brothers. Furthermore, yet another twenty-five per cent of the work is lost by constructing buildings which are unnecessary for the apostolate. Gossip should never be allowed and we shouldn't waste our time building so many houses. People will then be apostles, one hundred per cent.

964 Pray for the priests of today, and for those who are to come, that they may really love their fellow men, every day more and without distinction, and that they may know also how to make themselves loved by them.

965 I have been thinking of all the priests throughout the world. Help me to pray for the fruitfulness of their apostolates.

–"My brother in the priesthood, please speak always about God and, when you really do belong to him, your conversations will never be monotonous."

966 Preaching – the preaching of Christ *crucified* – is the word of God.

Priests need to prepare themselves as best they can before carrying out such a divine ministry, the aim of which is the salvation of souls.

Lay people should listen with very special respect.

967 It made me very happy to hear what they said about that priest: "He preaches with all his soul... and with his body too."

968 Let this be your prayer, apostolic soul: Lord, may I know how to *lean on* people and get them all to burn like fires of Love, which will then become the driving force of all our undertakings.

969 We Catholics have to go through life being apostles, with God's light and God's salt. We should have no fear, and we should be quite natural; but with so deep an interior life and such close union with Our Lord that we may shine out, preserving ourselves from corruption and from darkness, and spread around us the fruits of serenity and the effectiveness of Christian doctrine.

970 The sower went out to sow, to scatter the seed at all the crossroads of this earth. What a blessed task we have. We have the job of making sure that in all the circumstances of time and place the word of God takes root, springs up and bears fruit.

971 *Dominus dabit benignitatem suam et terra nostra dabit fructum suum* – the Lord will grant his blessing and the earth will bring forth its fruit.

That blessing is indeed the source of

all good fruit, the necessary climate for producing saints, men and women of God, in this world of ours.

Dominus dabit benignitatem – the Lord will grant his blessing. Notice, however, that he goes on to point out that he awaits our fruit – yours and mine. Nor is this crop to be meagre or blighted because we have not really given ourselves completely. He expects abundant fruit since he fills us with his blessings.

972 You saw your vocation like one of those pods that contain the seeds. The moment to expand will come and then the seeds will spread out and take root all at once.

973 You are to be yeast within the great multitudes that make up humanity – remember we are interested in all souls. In this way, with God's grace and your own correspondence to it, you will act as leaven throughout the world, adding quality, flavour and volume to the bread of Christ so that it can nourish the souls of others.

974 The enemies of Jesus – and even

some who call themselves his friends – come decked out in the armour of human knowledge and wielding the sword of power. They laugh at us Christians, just as the Philistine laughed at David and despised him.

In our own days too, the Goliath of hatred, the Goliath of falsehood, of dominating power, of secularism and indifferentism, will also come crashing to the ground. And then, once the giant of those false ideologies has been struck down by the apparently feeble weapons of the Christian spirit – prayer, expiation and action – we shall strip him of his armour of erroneous doctrines, equipping our fellow men instead with true knowledge, with Christian culture and the Christian way of life.

975 In the campaigns against the Church there are many organizations which conspire together, sometimes going hand in hand with those who call themselves good. They influence people through newspapers, leaflets, satire, calumnies and spoken propaganda. They then take people where they wish – to hell itself. They try to turn people into an amorphous mass, as if they had no soul. They are a pitiful sight.

However, since people do have souls, we have to snatch them out of the claws of these organizations of evil and place them at the service of God.

976 Quite a considerable proportion of the people who go to Church read bad publications...

Calmly and with love of God we need to pray and teach them sound doctrine so that they don't go on reading those diabolical worthless papers, which they claim their families buy – for they are ashamed of it – though perhaps it is they themselves who do so.

977 Defend the truth with charity and firmness when the things of God are at stake. Practise holy shamelessness in denouncing errors, even though at times they are no more than insinuations; at other times they will be odious utterances of the most blatant ignorance, and, normally, a sign of man's frustration at not being able to endure the fruitfulness of the word of God.

978 In times of general confusion it may seem as though God is not listening to your pleading with him on behalf of *his* souls, and is turning a deaf ear to your calls. You even reach the point of thinking that all your apostolic labours have been in vain.

–Don't worry! Carry on working with the same cheerfulness, the same energy, the same zeal. Allow me to insist: when you work for God, *nothing* is unfruitful.

979 My child, all the seas of this world are ours and the places where it is harder to fish are the places where it is all the more necessary.

980 Through your Christian doctrine, your upright life and your work well done, you have to give good example to the people around you – relatives, friends, colleagues, neighbours, pupils – in the way you carry out your profession and fulfil the duties your job entails. You cannot be a shoddy worker.

981 That close intimacy you have with

Christ means that you have a duty to bear fruit.

–And yours will be a fruit that will satisfy the hunger of men who come up to you in your work, in your day-to-day life, in your family environment...

982 When you fulfil your duties in a cheerful and generous way you obtain abundant grace from God for other souls also.

983 Make an effort to spread your Christian spirit to the world about you, so that there may be many friends of the Cross.

984 As well as having given you abundant and effective grace, the Lord has given you a brain, a pair of hands and intellectual powers so that your talents may yield fruit.

God wants to work miracles all the time – to raise the dead, make the deaf hear, restore sight to the blind, enable the lame to walk... – through your sanctified professional work, which you will have turned into a holocaust that is both pleasing to God and useful to souls.

985 The day you no longer strive to draw others closer to God – since you ought to be a burning coal all the time – you will become a contemptible little piece of charcoal, or a little heap of ashes to be scattered by the slightest puff of wind.

–You have to be on fire; you need to be a thing that burns, producing flames of the love of God, of faithfulness and apostolate.

986 Invoke the Blessed Virgin. Keep asking her to show herself a Mother to you – *monstra te esse Matrem!* As well as drawing down her Son's grace, may she bring the clarity of sound doctrine to your mind, and love and purity to your heart, so that you may know the way to God and take many souls to him.

Eternity

987 A son of God fears neither life nor death, because his spiritual life is founded on a sense of divine filiation. God is my Father, he thinks, and he is the Author of all good; he is all Goodness.

–But, you and I, do we really act as sons of God?

988 I was delighted to see that you understood what I had said to you: you and I have to work and live and die like people in love, and we will *live* in this way for all eternity.

989 God always wins. If you are his instrument, you too will win, because you will fight God's battles.

990 Sanctity consists precisely in this: in struggling to be faithful throughout your life and in accepting joyfully the Will of God at the hour of death.

991 When you receive Our Lord in the Holy Eucharist, thank him from the bottom of your heart for being so good as to be with you.

Have you ever stopped to consider that it took centuries and centuries before the Messiah came? All those patriarchs and prophets praying together with the whole people of Israel: Come, Lord, the land is parched!

If only your loving expectation were like this.

992 Even in our times, despite those who deny God, earth is very close to Heaven.

993 You wrote: "*Simile est regnum caelorum* – the Kingdom of God is like a treasure... This passage from the Holy Gospel has fallen on my soul and taken root. I had read it so many times before, without grasping its meaning, its divine flavour."

Yes, everything! The prudent man has to sell everything to obtain the treasure – the precious pearl of Glory.

994 Talk with Our Lady and tell her trustingly, O Mary, in order to live the ideal which God has set in my heart I need to fly very high – ever so high!

It is not sufficient to detach yourself, with God's help, from the things of this world, recognising them as the merest clay. More is needed: even if you were to put the whole universe in a pile under your feet to get closer to Heaven... it wouldn't suffice!

You have to fly, without the support of anything here on earth, relying on the voice and the inspiration of the Spirit. And you will tell me: But my wings are stained and smeared with the clinging mud of many years.

And I repeat: Turn to Our Lady. Mary, you should say to her again, I can hardly get off the ground. The earth draws me like an accursed magnet. Mary, you can make my soul take off on that glorious and definitive flight which has as its destination the very Heart of God.

–Trust in her, for she is listening to you.

995 Think how pleasing to God Our Lord is the incense burnt in his honour. Think also how little the things of this earth are worth; even as they begin they are already ending.

In Heaven, instead, a great Love awaits you, with no betrayals and no deceptions. The fullness of love, the fullness of beauty and greatness and knowledge... And it will never cloy: it will satiate, yet still you will want more.

996 With a supernatural outlook, with serenity and peace. That is the way to see things, people and events – from the viewpoint of eternity.

And then, whatever barrier blocks your way – even if it is, humanly speaking, enormous – when you really raise your eyes to Heaven, how tiny it becomes!

997 If we are close to Christ and are following in his footsteps, we will wholeheartedly love poverty, privation and detachment from earthly things.

998 In our spiritual life, we often have to be ready to lose on earth so as to win in Heaven. This way we always win.

999 Men lie when they say “forever” in temporal matters. The only true “forever”, in the complete sense, is the *forever* of eternity.

–And that is the way you have to live, with a faith that brings a foretaste of the sweet honey of Heaven whenever you think about that eternity which is truly everlasting.

1000 If this were the only life we had, life would be a cruel joke. It would be hypocrisy, evil, selfishness, betrayal.

1001 Keep going forward cheerfully and trying hard, even though you are so little – nothing at all!

–When you are with Him nobody in the world can stop you. Consider, moreover, how everything is good for those who love God. Everything in this world can be put right, except death, and for us death is Life.

1002 To save mankind, Lord, you died

on the Cross. And yet for *one* mortal sin you condemn a man to a hapless eternity of suffering. How much sin must offend you, and how much I ought to hate it!

1003 Saint Teresa assures us that "anyone who doesn't pray doesn't need any devil to tempt him; while whoever prays, even if only for a quarter of an hour each day, will necessarily be saved." This is because our conversation with Our Lord – who is so loving, even in times of difficulty or dryness of soul –enables us to see things in their proper perspective and discover the true proportions of life.

Be a soul of prayer.

1004 "So you are a king?"... Yes, Christ is the King, the King who not only grants you an audience whenever you like, but even in the madness of his love "gives up" – you know what I mean – his magnificent palace in Heaven, which you cannot yet reach, and waits for you in the Tabernacle.

–Don't you think it is absurd not to hurry to speak to him, and not to do so more assiduously?

1005 I am every day more convinced that happiness in Heaven is for those who know how to be happy on earth.

1006 With crystal clarity I see the formula, the secret of happiness, both earthly and eternal. It is not just a matter of accepting the Will of God but of embracing it, of identifying oneself with it – in a word, of loving the Divine Will with a positive act of our own will.

–This, I repeat, is the infallible secret of joy and peace.

1007 How often you will find yourself inundated, intoxicated with God's grace – and what a sin if you do not respond!

1008 In the hour of temptation, practise the virtue of Hope, saying: For my rest and enjoyment I have the whole of eternity ahead of me. Here and now, full of Faith, I will earn my rest through work and win my joy through suffering. What will Love be like in Heaven?

Better still, you should practise your Love by saying: What I want is to please my God, my Love, by doing his Will in all things, as though there were neither reward nor punishment –simply to please him.

1009 Whenever the worrying thought enters your head that you lack rectitude of intention – sometimes it may come like a flash of lightning, at other times like a filthy pestering fly which you brush off but which keeps coming back – always make contrary acts straight away... and carry on working calmly for Him and with Him.

–At the same time, even though you might feel you are only pronouncing the words mechanically, say slowly: Lord, I want nothing for myself. May everything be for your glory and for your Love.

1010 It is all the same to you, you tell me, to be here or in China.

–Well then, try to be always where you are fulfilling the Holy Will of God.

1011 Much depends on you too. If you respond many will remain in darkness no longer, but will walk instead along paths that lead to everlasting life.

1012 Get into the habit of praying to the Guardian Angel of each person you are following up, to help them to be good and faithful and cheerful, so that when the time comes they will be able to receive the eternal embrace of Love from God the Father, God the Son, God the Holy Spirit and from the Blessed Virgin.

1013 Like the grain of wheat, we too have to die in order to become fruitful.

You and I, with the help of God's grace, want to open up a deep furrow, to blaze a trail. That is why we have to leave behind our poor animal man and launch out into the sphere of the spirit, giving a supernatural meaning to every human undertaking and, at the same time, to all those engaged in them.

1014 Jesus, let my distractions be the other way round. Instead of recalling the world when I am engaged in conversation with you, let me rather recall you when I am engaged in the things of this world.

1015 You became a bit frightened

when you saw so much light, so bright that you thought it would be difficult to look, or even to see.

–Disregard your obvious weaknesses, and open the eyes of your soul to faith, to hope and to love. Carry on, allowing yourself to be guided by God through whoever directs your soul.

1016 Be generous. Don't ask Jesus for even one consolation!

–You ask me why. And I reply, because you know very well that even though this God of ours seems to be far away, he really is seated in the very centre of your soul, imparting a divine character to your whole life.

1017 I was saying to you that even people who had not received baptism were moved when they were telling me, "I can well understand that saintly souls must be happy, for they look at events with a vision that is above the things of this world. They see things with the eyes of eternity."

May you not lack that same vision, I added afterwards, so that you can respond to the special love with which the Blessed Trinity has treated you.

1018 I assure you that if we want to, as children of God, we can make a powerful contribution towards lighting up the work and the lives of men with the divine and eternal splendour which it has pleased the Lord to place in our souls.

But "he who says he abides in Jesus ought to walk the same way He walked" as Saint John teaches. It is a path which always leads to glory. But it also always passes through sacrifice.

1019 What a disappointment awaited those who saw the light of the pseudo-apostle, and wishing to come out of their darkness, were drawn to his light. They raced to get there. They may have left shreds of their skin along the way. Some in their eagerness for that light may also have left behind some shreds of their very souls. And now, having reached the pseudo-apostle, they find cold and darkness. Cold and darkness which will eventually fill the broken hearts of those who for a while have believed in that ideal.

It is an evil deed the pseudo-apostle has done. Those disappointed men who had been ready to give the flesh of their hearts in exchange for those glowing fires, for a breathtaking ruby of charity, drop once more back to the earth from which they had come. Down they go, with no fire in their heart, with a heart that is not a heart – just a chunk of ice shrouded in a darkness that will eventually cloud their brain.

You false apostle of paradoxes, see what you have done: because Christ is on your lips but not in your deeds; because you attract with a light which you yourself lack; because there is no warmth of charity in you, and you claim to be concerned about outsiders while all the time you are neglecting your own; because you are a liar, and *the devil* is the father of lies. And so, you are working for the devil, causing bewilderment to those who follow the Master, and even though you may triumph frequently here on earth, woe to you on that day which is approaching when our friend Death will come, and you shall see the anger of the Judge whom you have never deceived. Paradoxes, no, Lord: paradoxes? Never!

1020 This is the sure way: through humiliation to the Cross; then, from the Cross, with Christ, to the immortal Glory of the Father.

1021 How much I savoured the epistle of that day! The Holy Spirit through Saint Paul teaches us the secret of immortality and of Glory. All of us human beings yearn to live on.

We would wish to make those moments in our lives when we are happy last forever. We would wish the memory of our deeds to be glorified. We would like our cherished ideals to become immortal. And so it is that when we seem to be happy, when something consoles us in our distress, we all naturally say and desire that it should last forever, forever.

Oh the wisdom of the devil! How well he knew the human heart. You will be like gods, he said to our first parents. That was a cruel deception. Saint Paul in this Epistle to the Philippians teaches us a divine secret by which to attain immortality and Glory: Jesus... emptied himself, taking the form of a slave... He humbled himself and became obedient unto death, even death on the Cross. Therefore God has highly exalted him and bestowed on him a name which is above every other name, that at the name of Jesus every knee should bow, in Heaven and on earth and under the earth...

1022 If we are to accompany Christ in his Glory, in his final triumph, we have first of all to share in his holocaust, becoming identified with him, who died on Calvary.

1023 Don't let yourself be distracted, don't give free rein to your imagination. Live the life within you and you will be closer to God.

1024 Help me repeat in the ear of this person and of that other one... and of everyone: a sinner who has faith, even if he were to obtain all the blessings of this earth, will necessarily be unhappy and wretched.

It is true that the motive that leads us

(and should lead everyone) to hate sin, even venial sin, ought to be a supernatural one: that God abhors sin from the depths of his infiniteness, with a supreme, eternal and necessary hatred, as an evil opposed to the infinite good. But the first reason I mentioned to you can lead us to this other one.

1025 You will have as much sanctity, as you have mortification done for Love.

1026 Violent persecution had broken out. And that priest prayed: Jesus, may every sacrilegious fire increase in me the fire of Love and Reparation.

1027 When you consider the beauty, the greatness and the effectiveness of apostolic work, you affirm that your head aches thinking of the amount of ground that still has to be covered – there are so many souls who are waiting! And you feel so very happy offering yourself as a slave to Jesus. You have a great desire for his Cross and for suffering, for Love and for souls. Without thinking about it, in an instinctive movement– which was one of Love – you stretched out your arms and opened the palms of your hands, ready for him to nail you to his Holy Cross. You were ready to be his slave – *serviam* – which is to reign.

1028 I was moved by the heartfelt petition that came from your lips: "My God, my only desire is to be pleasing in your sight; nothing else matters to me. My Mother Immaculate, may I be motivated exclusively by Love."

1029 With your whole heart, ask for death, and a thousand deaths, rather than offend your God.

And not because of the punishment due to sin, which we deserve so much, but because Jesus has been and is so good to you.

1030 My God, when will I love you for yourself? Although when we think about it, Lord, to desire an everlasting reward is to desire you, for you give yourself as our reward.

1031 Taste and see that the Lord is good, the Psalmist says.

–Spiritual conquest, which is Love, has

to be – in big things and small – a desire for the Infinite, for eternity.

1032 Jesus, I don't want to think of what "tomorrow" will be like, for I don't want to put limits on your generosity.

1033 Make those reflections of your friend your own. He wrote: "I was considering how good God was to me and, full of interior joy, I was ready to shout out loud, there in the street, for everyone to know about my filial gratitude: 'Father! Father!' And though not in fact shouting out loud, I kept calling him so – 'Father!' – in a low voice, many times, quite certain that it pleased him.

–I seek nothing else. I only want to please him and give him Glory. Everything for him. If I desire my salvation and my sanctification it is because I know that he desires it. If in my Christian life I hunger for souls, it is because I know that he has this great hunger. I say this in all truth: I will never set my sights on the prize. I don't desire a reward: everything for Love!"

1034 How that sick woman whom I tended spiritually loved the Will of God! She saw her many, long-lasting and painful illnesses (not a single part of her body was healthy), as a blessing from Jesus and a sign of his special love. Although in her humility she used to say that she deserved punishment, the terrible sufferings that she felt all over her were not a punishment, but a mercy.

–We spoke of death. And of Heaven. And of what she was going to say to Jesus and to Our Lady. And how she would be "working" much more from up there than she could down here. She was ready to die whenever God wanted... but, she exclaimed, full of joy, "If only it could be today!" She looked forward to death with the same joy as one who knows that when we die we go to meet our Father.

1035 Do not fear death. Death is your friend!

–Try to get used to the fact of death: peer into your grave often, looking at and smelling, and touching your own rotting corpse there, a week, no more, after your death.

–Remember this especially when you are troubled by the impulses of your flesh.

1036 When he bared his soul to me he said, "These days I have been thinking about death as a rest, in spite of my crimes. And I thought that if I was told: 'The time has come for you to die', I would gladly reply: 'The time has come for me to Live'."

1037 To die is a good thing. How can anyone with faith be, at the same time, afraid to die? But as long as the Lord wants to keep you here on earth, it would be cowardice for you to want to die. You must live, live and suffer and work for Love: that is your task.

1038 At least once a day, cast your mind ahead to the moment of death so that you can consider the events of each day in this light.

I can assure you that you will have a good experience of the peace this consideration brings.

1039 You became very serious when you heard me say: I accept death whenever God wants it, the way he wants it, where he wants it; and at the same time I think it is *too easy* to die early, because we should want to work many years for him, and because of him, in the service of others.

1040 To die?... That's too easy, I say once more.

–Say, just as that holy bishop did when he was old and sick, *non recuso laborem* – Lord, as long as I can be useful, I do not refuse to keep on living and working for you.

1041 You shouldn't want to do things to gain merit, nor out of fear of the punishments of purgatory. From now on, and always, you should make the effort to do everything, even the smallest things, to please Jesus.

1042 Desire ardently that, when that unavoidable good sister of yours, death, comes to render you the service of taking you to God, she will not find you attached to anything on this earth!

1043 If you long to have life – eternal life and happiness –you must not leave the barque of Holy Mother Church. Look, if you go beyond the confines of the ship you end up in the waves of the sea, heading for death, drowned in the ocean. You cease to be with Christ. You lose that friendship of his which you freely chose when you realised that it was he who was offering it to you.

1044 Jesus came down to this earth to suffer... and so that others might avoid sufferings, even earthly ones.

1045 There is no greater self-mastery than to know oneself to be serving, in a willing service of all souls!

–This is how to gain the greatest honours, both on earth and in Heaven.

1046 In the face of suffering and persecution, a certain soul with supernatural sense said, "I prefer to take a beating down here rather than get it in purgatory."

1047 If I love, there will be no hell for me.

1048 How good it is to live on God's bounty! How good it is to desire nothing other than his Glory.

1049 If you really want to attain eternal life and honour, you must learn in many cases to put aside your own noble ambitions.

1050 Don't lay so much stress on '*my* health', '*my* family name', '*my* career', '*my* job', or '*my* next step'... How annoying this can be! It would seem you have forgotten that *you* don't have anything, that everything is *His*. How annoying this can be! It would seem you have forgotten that *you* don't have anything, that everything is *His*.

When sometimes – perhaps without reason – you feel humiliated; when you think your opinion should prevail; when you notice that at every moment your "self" keeps cropping up: your things, your things, your things... convince yourself that you are killing time, and that what you need is someone to *kill* your selfishness.

1051 I advise you not to look for

praise, even when you deserve it. It is better to pass unnoticed, and to let the most beautiful and noble aspects of our actions, of our lives, remain hidden. What a great thing it is to become little! *Deo omnis gloria!* –All the glory to God.

1052 In moments of disappointment, that soul said to Our Lord: "My Jesus, what else could I give you apart from my honour, if I had nothing else? If I had had a fortune I would have given it to you. If I had had virtues, I would have built up each one to serve you better. The only thing I had was my honour and I have given it to you. May you be blessed! It's clear that it was safe in your hands!"

1053 It is from clay I come and the earth is the inheritance of all my lineage.

Who but God deserves praise?

1054 When you feel self-love – pride! – stirring within you, making you out to be a superman, it is time to cry out: *No!* In this way you will savour the joy of the good son of God who goes through life with faults, but doing good.

1055 *Sancta Maria, Stella maris* – Holy Mary, Star of the sea, be our guide.

Make this firm request, because there is no storm which can shipwreck the most Sweet Heart of Mary. When you see the storm coming, if you get into that firm Refuge which is Mary, there will be no danger of your wavering or going down.

INDEX TO SCRIPTURAL REFERENCES‡

Part 1 Scripture references in *The Forge*

Old Testament

‡ This index is in two parts. The first part, divided according to the books of the Old and New Testaments, includes references to Scripture in *The Forge*. The second part, which follows the order of the points of *The Forge,* lists references to Scripture (explicit or implicit) in *The Forge*. As the author wrote before the Neo-Vulgate was published, reference is usually made to the Vulgate (for instance, the Psalms are numbered as in the Vulgate).

New Testament

Part 2 References to Scripture in *The Forge*

691 Eph (5:32)
694 Acts (1:1)
703 Gen (1:3-31)
708 Luke (2:51-52)
711 Matt (27:12,27-31)
711 Mark (15:16-19)
711 Mark (15:4-5)
711 John (19:1-3)
711 Luke (22:63-65)
711 Luke (23:2-9)
716 Ps (19:8)
753 Matt (26:41)
753 Mark (14:38)
754 Acts (9:6)
758 John (19:25)
764 Luke (23:26)
771 Luke (22:42)
786 Gal (2:19)
795 Matt (5:11)
795 Rom (15:13)
797 Ps (68:9-10)
799 Is (30:15)
803 1 Cor (4:13)
805 Matt (14:31)
807 John (2:3)
810 Luke (2:51)
818 John (14:6)
823 Matt (16:24)
823 Luke (9:23)
824 John (6:35)
839 1 Cor (4:20)
842 John (8:32)
848 Luke (16:8)
865 1 Tim (2:4)
866 Jer (31:3)
1031 Ps (33:9)
867 Matt (11:28)
869 Matt (22:37)
869 Mark (12:30-33)
869 Deut (6:5)
875 Jer (18:6)
881 1 Cor (6:20)
881 1 Pet (1:18-19)
882 1 Pet (2:9)
883 Luke (22:15)
889 John (13:34-35)
900 Rom (15:13)
901 Luke (4:40)
906 Matt (9:37)
906 Luke (10:2)
915 John (15:16)
917 Luke (19:17)
927 Is (60:8)
932 John (15:1-7)
945 1 Cor (6:20)
947 Luke (12:49)
953 1 Cor (9:22)
961 1 Cor (4:4)
970 Matt (13:3)
970 Mark (4:3)
970 Luke (8:5)
971 Ps (84:13)
974 1 Sam (17:42-44)
993 Matt (13:44-45)
1001 Rom (8:28)
1004 John (18:37)
1013 John (12:24)
1018 1 John (2:6)
1021 Gen (3:5)
1021 Phil (2:7-10)

General Index